THE FAILURE OF THE ROMAN REPUBLIC

THE FAILURE OF THE ROMAN REPUBLIC

BY

R. E. SMITH, M.A.
Professor of Ancient History in the University of Manchester

CAMBRIDGE
AT THE UNIVERSITY PRESS
1955

PUBLISHED BY
THE SYNDICS OF THE CAMBRIDGE UNIVERSITY PRESS

London Office: Bentley House, N.W. 1
American Branch: New York

Agents for Canada, India, and Pakistan: Macmillan

Printed in Great Britain at the University Press, Cambridge
(Brooke Crutchley, University Printer)

PREFACE

Every μέν has its δέ, and every general statement its exception. I have attempted in the following pages to explain and interpret the failure of Roman society in the first century B.C., to show how this failure came about, and what were its effects upon the spirit of the society. In doing this I have described what I believe to have been the characteristics of this society in its time of disintegration. But I am well aware that, while the general tone may have been as I have described it, yet there were many men who were exceptions, men whose qualities of character and moral strength would have made them fit citizens of that earlier Rome from which the society of the first century had on the whole fallen so miserably away; there are, after all, few societies which could hope to equal the dismal record of Sodom. These exceptions have not found a place in this book, simply because I believe that they were exceptions, and that to infer the character of a society from its exceptions would be fallacious and futile; their existence must always be borne in mind, but their effect on their society during these times was too slight; they did not represent the grain of the wood.

Since the book is an interpretation of the history of Rome of the first century B.C., not an inquiry into the details of that history, the references are few, and the bibliography does not attempt to list all the works which I have put under contribution or which deal with the history and the other aspects of the subject; it is merely a guide to a student who may wish to pursue further the study of those aspects. To have referred to all the works to which I am indebted would have cluttered up the pages without adding strength to the interpretation; for the interpretation must stand or fall as a whole and does not depend on the detailed elucidation of any point or points; while detailed bibliographies are to be found in the many scholarly works which deal with the history, literature, etc., of the period.

Preface

I gladly take this opportunity of expressing my gratitude to two scholars and friends, whose help, encouragement and criticism have been continuous from the inception of this book until it took its final shape, Professor Sir Frank E. Adcock, and Dr A. H. McDonald. Their agreement was encouraging, their disagreement stimulating; their knowledge and advice helped me to remove many inaccuracies and distortions. The final product owes a very great deal to both of them, though for the views expressed I must accept the sole responsibility, since I know that they do not win their full acceptance. I also gladly here record the pleasure and profit I derived from my many conversations on society and the place of religion in society with the Reverend Professor J. McIntyre, of St Andrew's College, Sydney; I learnt much from them and crystallized my own views. And finally I must thank the Syndics of the Cambridge University Press, the readers, and all those responsible, for their very great courtesy, advice and helpfulness from the moment the manuscript was in their hands; if there are still any errors or mistakes, the fault is entirely mine.

R.E.S.

MANCHESTER
January 1955

CONTENTS

PART I

ROME, 200–140 B.C.

PART II

THE CONSEQUENCES OF VICTORY

PART III

THE POLITICAL DISRUPTION

PART IV

THE CONSEQUENCES OF DISINTEGRATION

FRONTISPIECE

The illustration shows a bas-relief from an altar or the base for a group of statues, of the late 2nd or 1st century B.C., dedicated by a Cn. Domitius Ahenobarbus, who may, depending on the interpretation of the scene to the left of the altar, most probably be identified as the censor of 115 B.C. or the associate of Antony during the Civil War. The scene may represent the taking of the census, the enrolment of colonists (for Narbo Martius) or of volunteers (for Marius' army), or the discharge of soldiers. However this may be, we see the god Mars in military dress standing to left of the altar, to right a figure in civilian dress (Cn. Domitius Ahenobarbus?) pouring a libation, while attendants bring up the animals for the traditional sacrifice, the *suovetaurilia*, an Italian religious rite of considerable antiquity.

PART I

ROME, 200–140 B.C.

It is intended in the following chapters to give only the general character of Roman society and government during these years, in order to be able to show the conditions at the time of Gracchi, the general tenor of their approach to their problems, both social and imperial, and the effect of the Gracchi upon this society.

NOTE

References and very short notes are printed as footnotes. All other notes are printed in the section beginning on p. 169. The reader is referred to these by an asterisk (*) in the text.

INTRODUCTION

The failure of the Roman Republic as a spiritual and political force, its incapacity to rule the Empire it had created, and its catastrophic end will continue to exercise a lively interest among students of history as long as men continue to be interested in the study of human societies, and strive to extract from the failures and successes of the past some hint or lesson which will help them better to understand the mysterious workings of men in society. Many men in many ages have sought to explain the inexplicable, and their explanations have sprung largely from the atmosphere of their contemporary age. We shall never fully explain why the Republic fell, because we can never wholly translate ourselves into the minds of those Romans who acted out the play; but some times are more closely akin than others to the Roman atmosphere, and with sympathetic imagination a man in such an age may hope to feel the Roman crisis more nearly than his great-grandfather or great-grandson could expect to do. The fifty years before the First World War were quite alien to the Republic's crisis; men lived in a stable world, where law and order stretched to its uttermost bounds, and where difference or disagreement was resolved according to the claims of sweet reason; they enjoyed a feeling of solidity and permanence, which encouraged them to suppose that, as things were, so they would always be, with such modifications and adjustments as 'Progress' would undoubtedly suggest. To them the Roman problem was a political one, soluble in political terms, to be explained by supposing that at a particular time the wrong political move was made. The time and paper consumed in deciding 'quis iustius induit arma'* well illustrates this; that to them was the problem; they thought that if they could show how the opposing chessmen had come to be in their present squares, and which player, if either, had cheated, they had resolved the problem. It was seen in a coldly rational way, as they saw their own contemporary problems; how or why the grim game of human chess had ever been devised and started, how or why both sides were agreed that if they lost this game there could never be a return match, these were questions that left them unmoved; to have decided the legal responsibility was to have resolved everything.

We live in less certain times; all that they assumed as permanent we have either lost or fear to lose at any time. We are aware of problems where politics enter only as part of something bigger and more terrifying; we know that Westminster is but the mirror reflecting only the external form, that what we seek is buried deep within that form and will never be found by gazing merely on its outward shape; we know that institutions can be used by enemies to bring about the destruction of those very institutions; in the uncertainty and frustration which surround us we are aware that things happen without our deliberate willing, and even against our willing. It is what I may call the spiritual element which we see to be so important, transcending far political or economic issues, though often we allow our inner dissatisfaction to attach itself to one of these, hoping that some panacea will put to rout that dissatisfaction; but at least we know what it is to be unhappy and uncertain, without a certain means of remedy; and having seen so many nations flout the moral code our grandfathers believed to have been established for all time, having lost some of our confidence in it, we can feel with greater sympathy than they the Roman crisis, can appreciate with understanding their attempts to grapple with it, albeit in vain, can feel more keenly what Cicero and Varro were striving to accomplish, and can perhaps, even though our verdict must be unfavourable, say something in the summing up to indicate that we are not so sure we could have handled matters better.

The story of the hundred years 133–31 B.C. is the story of a failure, sudden and complete, clamped between two long periods of successful achievement, such that the failure seems to be both progeny and progenitor of success. It is this which gives the period such fascination for the student of human affairs; no facile, question-begging label of 'decadence' can explain a century which gave birth to the Roman Empire; inability to rise from the cradle of the city-state to the responsibility of world-empire is no explanation of Rome, as it might have been for the city-states of Greece; for the genius of Rome could and did meet the challenge. Rome's latent qualities of genius lay dormant, drugged by some narcotic power, while State and individuals grew steadily worse; then suddenly, as though at the kiss of the prince in the fairy-tale, she awoke to the fulfilment of her destiny after the nightmare of the first century B.C. This book attempts to suggest at least in part how this came about, and how the causes which brought the Republic to its unmourned end* were working equally within every part of society and reflected themselves in all the Romans said or did.

It may seem strange to begin this task in 200 B.C., but there is a good reason. The main thesis of this study is that the Gracchi by the means they adopted in pursuit of their ends precipitated a spiritual crisis in Rome which was the first cause of all that followed. In order therefore to show the nature of the crisis we must first glance at the general tenor of Rome's history in the preceding years. The year 200 B.C. suggests itself as the *terminus a quo*; it marked the end of Rome's struggle with Carthage, and the beginning of that epoch which was to see Rome's power paramount throughout the Mediterranean. We shall study for our purpose only the general character of the Senatorial government during these years, and note with what sense of duty and responsibility, with what measure of success the Senate addressed itself to its many problems.

CHAPTER I

THE POLITICAL UNITY

This is the age of Senatorial government. Throughout these years the Senate exercised a supreme control over the destinies of Rome in foreign and domestic affairs. For this there were obvious reasons; its handling of the Hannibalic War had rightly given it a claim to respect and obedience; it was the only permanent assembly in Rome capable of formulating and carrying out policy, of dealing with foreign ambassadors, of handling the State's finances; and within it was collected the whole wisdom and experience of the State. It governed by reason of its fitness to govern, and no one thought to challenge its supremacy.

The Senate consisted at this time of 300 members, but the effective control of affairs was within the hands of a small group of this body, the *nobiles*. The old distinction between patrician and plebs had long ceased to have any importance; in its place had grown up a group of families whose ancestors had attained to consular rank; the attainment of this office conferred nobility on the family, whose descendants were known as *nobiles*. Beneath them and less exclusive were the families who had attained praetorian rank. Access to the consulship was jealously guarded by the *nobiles*; for a *novus homo* to win his way to the office was exceedingly rare, and, without the active support of some group of the *nobiles*, impossible. How tight a hold they kept upon the consulship the figures for these years show; during the 100 years preceding the tribunate of Tib. Gracchus, out of 200 consulships 159 went to 26 families, 99 of them to only 10 families. Between 200 and 146 B.C. only 4 *novi homines* forced their way to the highest office, all of them helped by some section of the *nobiles*. The figures for the praetorship tell a not very different tale, though not within quite such narrow restrictions. It followed that the effective power was in the hands of a few families, and that the chief function of the humbler members was to support one or other of the leading personages.

The nobles enjoyed very great power, based upon their control of the Senate, of the elections and of the priesthoods. With this control their power was absolute, and the only restriction in fact was the rivalry between their own contesting groups. The political history of these years is the history of these competing groups, clustered round some great noble family, which for a time exercises the chief control of the State, and puts into execution its own foreign and domestic policy. They controlled through the Senate all policy, the relations of Rome with foreign powers, her policy with respect to expansion, her finances, her economic and social development, and as senior magistrates they governed Rome and her provinces, and commanded her armies.

The people, who formed the assemblies that elected the magistrates and composed the legionary armies that made Rome's conquests, enjoyed a theoretical rather than a real power. They did vote for the election of magistrates and pass laws; but they elected from among a small number of the aristocracy, who alone normally presented themselves for office, and they passed only those measures which magistrates or tribunes proposed, and what they proposed was usually what the Senate approved of. Very many of them were *clientes* of some noble, who was their *patronus*. The *cliens-patronus* relationship was very old in Rome, and had originally been a means of providing protection to someone who was outside the law, in return for certain services and the sacred duty of helping the *patronus* in time of need. The *patronus* still helped his *cliens* economically, if necessary, by giving him work or a piece of land, or by helping him in a political career. In return the *cliens* was expected to support his *patronus* in his political life, by casting his vote in accordance with his patron's wishes. Those that were not clients of any noble were often bribed to cast their votes in a particular way.* The possession of the vote therefore either provided a means of doing a service or of making money by its sale; it was not regarded as a valued responsibility to be exercised as conscience and reason dictated. The people really had no place in politics; they did not understand the intricacies of government, nor did they wish to try their hand at it. They were well content to leave it to 'the quality', who had both the wish and the knowledge.

The Equites, whose rise to importance began now and continued during the next fifty years, were the business men of the community. As government contractors, as financiers, and as business men plying their business in many parts of the world, they became a rich and influential class; but they took no direct part in government. Their votes in the centuries could be important, and the influence of their wealth could be great; but they did not wish to share the responsibilities of government, preferring to give their time to business. As their importance increased, their relations with the nobles became strained; business interests not seldom clashed with the nobles' policy, and the nobles tried with lessening success to thwart them. As their interests expanded, they were anxious to influence policy without becoming partners in government.

But while there was a certain strain in the later years between the nobles and the Equites, yet the position of the Senate was unshaken. The nobles controlled government, and the other sections of Rome were well content. It was a true aristocratic society, with all the strength and by no means all the weakness of such, and the society which they controlled was an integrated society, in which the different classes respected the position of the others without the bitter hatred which develops when a society splits into groups. With all classes the State came first; they pursued their own interests, yet, if there was a conflict between the two, the State won. All classes were loyal to their city-state, Rome, with whose ideals, as they found expression in the epic poem of Ennius, they felt themselves at one.

The feeling of destiny, of the gods' particular care of them for some purpose which as yet was undefined, was the feeling of

Roman society after the Hannibalic War.[1] It was essentially a religious society; the ordinary people still believed in their gods, and while some of the Hellenists may have begun to have first shadows of doubt, it was not general;* had it been so, the *Annales* would be incomprehensible. This is important; all integrated societies are founded on a religious faith, as though all classes felt they had a destiny imposed on them from outside, and this creates a true humility, a sense of their inadequacy without that outside help.* It was an age of slow, imperceptible change, wherein it was difficult to note any change in circumstances which called for a corresponding change in relationship; by 140 B.C. the difference in circumstances was clear, and it called for a readjustment of relations.

Not only within Rome itself was there mutual agreement among the classes, but between Rome and the Italians there was to be found a similar harmony in relationship. The governing classes of the Italian cities worked in close co-operation with the Roman Senate; they were loyal to Rome and the federation, and there was no important difference between the two.[2] Their governments were, like Rome's, aristocratic, but the evidence suggests that they ruled with the consent of their citizens, and that the harmony within their cities was, in the early part of this century, hardly less than that at Rome. It may be said of this period in general that it was a period of happiness for Rome and Italy, and that the governors, assured of their primacy, carried out their work with a responsibility which does them credit and a concern for Rome's well-being which acquits them of selfishness.

[1] See below, ch. IV, pp. 31 ff.

[2] See McDonald, *Cambridge Historical Journal*, VI (1939), 124 ff.; *J.R.S.* XXXIV (1944), 11 ff.

CHAPTER II

THE SOCIAL UNITY[1]

Before we discuss the aims and limitations of the domestic and foreign policy, it will be well to glance briefly at the concern shown by the nobles for the protection and defence of the *ethos* of their society. They felt themselves to be the guardians of that tradition of Romanism, the *mos maiorum*, which gave their society its peculiar and remarkable quality and its citizens their special character; that quality and character which had enabled them to surmount the Hannibalic threats and which, they believed, had come to them from Heaven.

The ideal of public service among the nobles was strong; it was at once their duty and responsibility and also the avenue to personal and family fame. Their family pride was great and was encouraged by the practice of lining the walls of the *atrium* with the *imagines* of their ancestors, with their achievements outlined on the *tituli* beneath them. The *laudationes*, the *elogia*, the funeral, at which the masks of the dead ancestors were worn in the procession, all contributed to make an individual aware that he was heir to the glory and the responsibility of something greater than himself. It was not sufficient to be oneself; one must be a Cornelius or a Fabius.[2] Their ideal of *virtus* is known to us from Ennius,* the *elogia* of the Scipios, the fragment of the *laudatio* of Metellus, and not least from the stories of early Rome in which they emphasized certain qualities of character in their heroes, courage, honesty, high sense of duty, obedience to the constituted authority, etc. It is perhaps best summed up in the fragment of Metellus' *laudatio*;[3] after cataloguing all his public offices it continues:

[1] I have incorporated in this and the following chapter parts of my Todd Memorial Lecture, *The Aristocratic Epoch of Roman Literature* (Sydney, 1947).

[2] See the story of Scipio Aemilianus in Polyb. XXXI, 23, 8 ff.

[3] Pliny, *Nat. Hist.* VII, 43, 139. This Metellus died in 221 B.C.

> Metellus wished to be a champion warrior, the best orator, the bravest general, to hold command in the greatest undertakings, to meet with highest official preferment, to be a leader in wisdom, to be deemed the leading Senator, to gain great wealth by honest means, to have many children, and to be the most distinguished man in the state. These things fell to his lot, and to the lot of no other man since the founding of Rome.[1]

The ideal of the noble is clear here: to be the leading man in the State in war and peace, to hold the highest office and the most important military command, to acquire wealth honourably and to have children to carry on the family. There is no need to labour the point; the sixth book of Polybius is a noble tribute to the qualities which made Rome great, and the nobles were both the possessors and the guardians of these qualities.

The *mos maiorum* was the foundation of Rome's society, the sum of all the customs, practices, training and education by which the Roman character had been developed, and to the maintenance of the *ethos* of Roman society the nobles paid particular attention. For although to only the nobles were the glories of a public career open, yet all classes had their place in society, which was one and indivisible, and undesirable novelties and influences in one section could only have a deleterious effect upon the whole. The society must be kept pure of taint, and only the governors could do that.

This period witnessed the great inrush of Hellenic influence in the form of literature, philosophy, art and by no means least the Greeks themselves. Such influences from without were not new to Rome; Etruria had profoundly influenced Rome in art, architecture and religion since the time of the kings; and though the influence of Etruria was no longer felt at Rome, she had learnt from this experience how to adopt and to adapt. More important for our purpose was the influence of Magna Graecia; this influence had been at first indirect, by way of Etruria and Southern Latium; but since the Pyrrhic War and the capture of Tarentum

[1] The translation is that of D. R. Stuart in *Epochs of Greek and Roman Biography*, 242.

Rome had come into direct contact with the highly developed Greek culture of Southern Italy, and from this contact had already learnt and absorbed much. During the Punic War Sicily had been one of the important theatres of combat; there the Roman army had been brought into close contact with a flourishing Greek civilization, and at Syracuse with a city which had attained a high level of culture, and whose buildings and private houses were of a beauty and luxury quite unknown at Rome. The story of Marcellus' sack of Syracuse, with the plunder and booty consisting of works of art of all kinds which was shipped to Rome, is sufficient to show that the work of the Greek artistic genius was not unknown to Rome by 200 B.C. Their earlier contact with an art and literature to which Rome had no counterpart had aroused among the better minds an appreciation for these things and made them ready to steep themselves more deeply in them should opportunity offer.

The literature of this period was the product of an educated class in a society that had come into contact with the culture of the Greek world, and having been attracted to it determined to create for Rome a literature which could be set beside that of Greece. It was the fate of Roman letters thus to come into contact with a literature so far beyond its own stage of development; for Rome's political maturity and importance had far outstripped her cultural development, and she could not hope or wish to be an important Mediterranean power and at the same time to set a cultural *cordon sanitaire* around Italy, in order that her own native products might grow to independent manhood.

In consequence the genius of Italy was stifled at an early stage; the nobles in 200 B.C. had eaten of the apple of knowledge and knew themselves to be culturally naked. In such a situation they did what alone they could, followed the *exemplaria Graeca*, and thus inaugurated a Latin literature which broke with its own rude past and by its pioneering efforts made possible the literature of future Rome with all its strength and weakness due to its original derivation from Greece. The literature they produced was in many elements artificial, as indeed it must have been, and it came abruptly to an end when Rome had sufficiently matured and developed her own personality; but it had served a useful and important purpose in hastening a literary maturity which must, if not stimulated from without, have come only with a far greater passage of time. On the other hand the break with its own native sources of inspiration remained almost complete; literature and the people remained separated; the metre, the language and the constructions of the people continued, to emerge in Medieval Latin; but except for occasional peeps the student of classical literature is hardly aware of their existence.

The literature of the second century was a social literature; its epic expressed the faith in Rome's destiny, its drama, connected like the Greek with the worship of the gods, provided a public and social form of entertainment. Its history, whether of the so-called annalists or of Cato, was written to subserve a public need, whether of informing an outside world of Rome and her intentions, or of inspiring a unity in Italy itself. The influence of Alexandria was but limited, and what was specifically Alexandrian was not to be found in second-century Rome. This is not surprising; Rome had developed to that stage where its society absorbed all a man's energy and loyalty; the individual was subordinated to the society and found his means of self-expression in his society and as a member of it. The individual, even if he were a Scipio, deferred to the group; and as men lived and thought in such an atmosphere, and were aware less of their individuality than of their membership of society, they did not look in upon themselves or concern themselves with the problems of the individual, and what we may style individual literature did not in consequence arise.

With the passage of the years interest in Greek thought and speculation grew; the nobles began to seek in reason a foundation for their social customs and beliefs, and the individual began to assume a position of greater importance. Panaetius' philosophy had a place for the individual as well as for society; the individual had a clear, inescapable moral duty towards his society, as did his society towards the world. The development of the individual within the society, and the discovery that the two need not conflict, was a natural accompaniment to Rome's growing maturity, aided as it was by contact with Greece. In Lucilius we have the first instance of an individual writer;* turning away from the specifically social literature of the immediate past, he recounts his own views and experiences, his moral strictures, his criticisms and literary judgements. Yet his individuality expresses itself within the framework of his society; where he criticizes, his criticisms are directed at those who have fallen from the standards of society, which are accepted and tacitly approved. In him we see the harmony between the individual and society, which it was the great work of Panaetius and Scipio to have achieved without loss to either. His appearance at this time has a certain symbolic quality, for the Gracchi, like himself, were in their individualism the product of their age; but he was in sympathy with, they in revolt against, their society. Scipio, who befriended Lucilius and uttered his curse over dead Tiberius,[1] knew wherein the difference lay; the individual must strengthen, not destroy, society.

Let us observe the nobles' attitude to literature, and first to poetry. We have seen that their ideal was one of public service; such an ideal left little opportunity for the professional poet, and in earlier times little chance to appreciate a poet's works. 'Men used not to respect the poet's art; anyone that gave attention to it or spent his time at parties was called a "vagabond".'[2] Thus wrote Cato in the first half of this century and the time to which he is referring is not a misty past but a comparatively recent one. The poet and the parasite at that time were equally the object of scorn and contempt. That attitude had changed; under the influence of Hellenism they had come to appreciate poetry, but they themselves did not engage in its composition. True, we find during this period aristocrats composing poems, such as Mum-

[1] Plutarch, *Tib. Gracch.* xx, 4.

[2] Gellius, xi, 2, 5.

mius, brother of him who sacked Corinth;[1] but they were not to be taken seriously; they were merely a sign of an educated man, one of his accomplishments. Suetonius tells us[2] that as a result of Crates' visit to Rome in 159 B.C. men dug from their obscurity old poems of their own or their friends, carefully revised them and read them before circles of friends for criticism and comment. The story is in itself sufficient to give us the picture of the amateur poets of the time, regarding verse-making as an educated refinement, at which it behoved the cultured man to try his hand. Suetonius[3] also tells us that apart from Scipio Aemilianus and Laelius, Q. Fabius Labeo, C. Sulpicius Galba and M. Popilius were all persons who might have helped Terence in writing his plays. This statement reveals two facts: first, that some aristocrats were thought to be competent poets; second, that though they were, it would have been unbecoming in them to produce plays under their own name, and that they would therefore have cloaked their Muse under the name of Terence.

But if such was their attitude towards the profession of poet in their own persons, they did not necessarily despise the poet as such, nor condemn his works. Livius had been the first Roman poet; he had translated the *Odyssey* into Saturnians, and had thus produced a national Italian epic.[4] Naevius and Ennius had gone further and produced, instead of Italian, Roman epics. All three had helped to bring their readers to a consciousness of their country, the latter two of their destiny and their inherent greatness. Livius also produced plays for the Roman stage; at this time the connexion between religion and the stage was close, and the production of plays was a contribution towards the changing ritual of Roman religion. He was called upon in the critical later stages of the Hannibalic War to write a religious hymn, and in token of his services to the State was founded what was later known as the Collegium Poetarum on the Aventine. We may see

[1] Cicero, *Ad. Att.* XIII, 6A.

[2] *De Gramm.* 2.

[3] *Life of Terence*, 4.

[4] See Altheim, *History of Roman Religion* (Eng. trans.), 297 ff.

from this that the nobility were not slow to reward the ex-slave for his service to the State.

It is not perhaps mere accident that many of the dramatists were non-Romans by birth, and some of them ex-slaves. That most of them depended on their success as playwrights or on patronage to eke out an existence, gave the governing class a hold on their work which they did not hesitate to exercise. The Romans themselves were unable to write plays at this time; the educated class turned deliberately away from the practice of letters, while the rest of Rome lived in an atmosphere of practical life which did not encourage the native genius to find expression in literature. Personal poetry does not flourish in a closely-welded society; there must be an atmosphere of individualism, even if it is in resistance to social restraints, before there can be individual expression; and at Rome in this period there was not that atmosphere. A foreigner may write a play for others; he cannot express their inmost thoughts for them. For epic too the atmosphere was no longer suitable. The defeat of Carthage had impressed the Romans no less than the rest of the world; they had felt that they were called to some destiny on this earth, and Naevius and Ennius had given expression to that feeling.[1] But that feeling was not now so vivid; true, many Romans were still conscious of a responsibility and a destiny; but amid the routine of office and Empire, with no death struggle or serious threat to stir them to a fresh consciousness of their ideals and to challenge an appraisal of their values, it was impossible that a new Roman epic should be born.

The nobles' attitude to poetry is clear: they would not give their own efforts to it, though they allowed others to, provided, as we shall see, that what they wrote supported or at least did not conflict with the *ethos* of Rome as they interpreted it. The *mos maiorum*, the Roman character and the underlying assumptions concerning the organization of the State and the duties of the different classes within it were alike topics about which there was

[1] See below, ch. IV, pp. 31 ff.

no compromise; support or silence was the only choice open to the poet; and it followed that the leading personalities were sacrosanct.

With prose the case was different. Latin prose was not at the beginning of our period the flexible instrument for expressing the whole gamut of human thought and emotions that it became with Cicero. It was stiff, unyielding, and was used chiefly for purposes of business and of State; there was a nascent oratory, hardly less stiff and unadorned. Men did not turn to this medium in which to express any but the most concrete of sentiments, for at this time their sentiments were all practical; theory had not begun to root itself at Rome. One form of prose composition did, however, develop during this period, that of historical composition. Rome, when she was engaged with Hannibal, felt the need to make her motives known to the world of Greece; and when that war was over, the need became even greater. Once they were inextricably involved with that world, whose culture they admitted to be superior to their own, and of whose good will they stood in need, the necessity to show the purity of their motives to nations brought up to believe only in wiles and tricks became even more pressing, especially when they wanted to be friendly—on their own terms —with parts at any rate of the Greek world. The Greeks were scornful of barbarians and lesser breeds; and those Greeks who had taken the trouble to try to understand Rome's motives had formed an adverse opinion of her intentions. The interpretation of Roman institutions in Rome and confederate institutions in Italy must therefore come from Rome; and since the aims and policy which required interpretation and explanation to the Greeks were those of the nobles who fashioned Roman policy, it was natural that the interpretation, too, should come from them. They alone had the secret and the wish, and hence arose that group of Senatorial historians who described for the Greek world in the Greek tongue Roman and Italian institutions and the Senatorial policy.

Family ambition found an outlet in these histories, and some of their authors did not scruple to exaggerate the achievements of their ancestors, perhaps at the expense of other families. But they restricted themselves to public life; their accounts were not embellished by sordid or fanciful stories of private life in the manner of some of the Greek historians; any distortion there might have been did not extend beyond the military and public achievements of rivals. Thus arose the one branch of letters to which the educated class gave their mind during this time, and that not primarily from a love of letters but from the strictly practical purpose of explaining their motives to a foreign world.*

CHAPTER III

RELIGION, THOUGHT AND LITERATURE

For the guardians of a close-knit society, whose *ethos* was based upon a *mos maiorum* that owed nothing to Greece, there could be a danger in the indiscriminate admission of foreign ideas and ways which might conflict with those of Rome. Such a conflict the nobles did not want and were determined to prevent. In all spheres of life, therefore, they exercised a vigilant censorship, aimed to exclude anything that might destroy the harmony of Roman society. Thought, religion and literature were the three doors through which the disintegrating influences could most easily enter, and these were therefore carefully guarded against unwanted intrusions.

In the realm of religion the Romans had always shown an easy tolerance in admitting new gods to their Pantheon. Polytheism, like polygamy, naturally tends to tolerance in new admissions; once multiplicity is accepted, without an upper limit there is no reason for excluding a fresh deity, if he seems likely to appeal to some worshippers; most Romans probably had their favourite god or goddess, and had no wish to deny to others a god of their choice. But the assumption always was that any new deity or any fresh religious practice, such as the *lectisternium*,[1] could be fitted into the society without conflicting with the *mos maiorum*; there must be no change in the religious attitude of their society. Such had been the attitude—probably unconscious—of Rome towards new gods. But there may be attached to a particular god a special form of worship, which requires the devotee to indulge in certain rites and rituals inimical to the established order. Hitherto Rome

[1] A Greek custom whereby a god or gods were invited to a meal, and couches provided for them.

had not had acquaintance with such gods, but in the early years of this period she became acquainted with two, and we may now turn to observe the nobles' reaction.

In 205 B.C. a fresh outburst of *religio* on the part of the people called for some action from the government.[1] The people had been prone to these outbursts during the Punic War, and the government had been compelled to resort to all sorts of religious contrivances to allay their panic. On this occasion they made their usual approach to the Sibylline books, and were told that they would drive the foreign foe from Italy if they brought to Rome the Idaean Mother from Pessinus. With great ceremony, therefore, in which the noble families took the leading part, the Magna Mater came to Rome, as it was thought, just another goddess. But very soon the Senate discovered that orgiastic rites were connected with her worship and they acted with prompt firmness; it was ordained by a *senatus consultum* that no Roman should take part in her worship.[2] The reason for this is clear; they had been quite ready to humour the people by the introduction of a fresh goddess, while they thought that her presence would not affect the Roman *ethos*; but when the unpleasant truth was discovered that connected with her worship were rites that conflicted with the *mos maiorum*, they at once sought to prevent its evil effects by banning the orgiastic ritual to Romans.

Again in 186 B.C. the Senate discovered that the worship of Dionysus had reached disquieting proportions throughout Italy; that in the course of this worship secret societies were formed, orgiastic ritual and immoral behaviour indulged in, and strange oaths taken.[3] The Senate again acted with speed and firmness; since secret societies tend in their very nature to be hostile to the society in which they are secret, and since these societies had foreign affiliations, the Senate was necessarily extremely worried. Regarding it as subversive activity, and considering such activity in social matters to be no less dangerous than in political, it pro-

[1] Livy, XXIX, 10 ff. [2] Dion. Hal. II, 19.

[3] The whole story is in Livy, XXXIX, 8 ff.

nounced the whole affair *coniuratio*, and with the help of the allies suppressed the worship, though those who wished to continue in the practice were allowed to do so, provided that not more than five persons collected in one group.[1]

We see in these two cases the Senate's attitude towards foreign religions when they were likely to infect society with an alien and antagonistic ritual. Another aspect of this attitude is seen in the suspension of the building of a permanent theatre in 157 B.C., at the instigation of Scipio Nasica. Theatres were still temporary structures erected near a temple for the showing of plays in connexion with a religious festival; the erection of a permanent theatre would therefore have two consequences: first, the connexion with the temple would be lost, and secondly, it would be possible to show plays at any time of the year instead of only on religious occasions. The erection of such a theatre would separate the stage from religion, and at a time when some men were uneasy at the relaxation of standards on the part of the people,[2] it was thought unwise to give encouragement to something which could lead to further dissoluteness. In consequence Rome never had a permanent theatre until Pompeius erected one in 55 B.C.

It may be said that this action confirms Polybius' interpretation of the nobles' attitude towards religion.[3] But caution is necessary here. There are degrees of belief, and even among men professing the same religion there is far from uniformity in the detail of what they believe. It is certain that the nobles' belief in the Roman religion was different from that of the uneducated *plebs*; but that does not mean that either group was insincere in its belief. It may be that to the student of religion the body of belief of the two groups represented almost different religions—that the Jupiter of the nobles and the Jupiter of the *plebs* had little in common but the name. We, however, are not considering the question as students

[1] Livy, XXXIX, 18, 9; S. C. de Bacch. XI, 19 ff. (in Riccobono, *Fontes Iuris anteiustiniani*, I, 241).

[2] See Gelzer, *Philologus*, XL (1931), 285 = *Vom Röm. Staat*, I, 107–8; Altheim, *op. cit.* 290–1.

[3] VI, 56, 6 ff.

of religion but as students of society; and from that point of view the common name is all-important; it was that which held the society together. True, the educated class may have felt that the *plebs* had but a crude, inadequate understanding of their gods, and that they must therefore go through certain motions which they were sure had little point, in order to satisfy the people and keep their allegiance to the society. But that does not mean that they did not themselves believe in those gods, even though they may have thought of them in a different and, in their own view, deeper way. Both groups believed in the same gods, the gods of their city and society, and without that common belief their society would not have held so firmly together.*

When society began to disintegrate, religion became political, and came to be used shamelessly for political purposes. It had always been political in the sense that it had an important place in political activities, and no doubt on occasions the auspices may have been put to political use.* But there is no evidence that this was commonly done at this time; our evidence is for the succeeding age. It is difficult to analyse human motives; sincerity and self-deception can sometimes combine to cheat the wisest man. Frequently one sees what one wants to see, and is then convinced that there was nothing else to see; but between that and cynicism there is a very wide gulf. To us it may seem that the nobles abused their religious powers between 200 and 140 B.C.; to the nineteenth-century world it seemed as though the English were hypocrites, because they always served their own advantage in the name of God. Yet the English were not hypocrites, for hypocrites do not die for their false protestations. They sincerely believed that they were doing God's will, and if their course of action proved profitable, that seemed to them just because they did carry out God's will. A mixture of sincerity and self-deception, perhaps; an honest belief certainly. Yet to outsiders, who were not part of that integrated society and its beliefs, it *was* hypocrisy; for since they could by reason demolish so absurd a claim, they supposed the English had done the same thing but pretended to believe it still.

We should not too lightly assume absence of true religion among the nobles; somehow they conducted themselves with an honesty and incorruptibility that drew the admiration of Polybius.*

In the realm of philosophy we find the Senate applying limitations similar to those they applied in religion. The better Romans were attracted to Greek philosophy; they sometimes made visits to Athens to meet the leading philosophers, and some acquaintance with Greek philosophy began to be a part of the education of a young noble. Yet in 161 B.C. philosophers and *rhetores* were banished from Rome,[1] and in 154 B.C. Diogenes, Critolaus and Carneades, who were representing Athens as ambassadors, were hustled untimely out of Rome, their business having been rushed through the Senate at Cato's instigation.[2] Yet about ten years later Panaetius, the distinguished Stoic, was to spend two years with Scipio, without protest from anyone.

A glance at Plutarch's description of the second incident will help us to understand the attitude of the nobles.[3]

> The charm [he says] of Carneades especially, which had boundless power, and a fame not inferior to his power, won large and sympathetic audiences and filled the city, like a rushing mighty wind, with the sound of his promises. Report spread far and wide that a Greek of amazing talent, who disarmed all opposition by the magic of his eloquence, had infused a tremendous passion into the youth of the city, in consequence of which they forsook their other pleasures and pursuits and were 'possessed' of philosophy.... Cato, at the very outset, when this zeal for discussion came pouring into the city, was distressed, fearing lest the young men, by giving this direction to their ambition, should come to love a reputation based on mere words more than one achieved by martial deeds. And when the fame of the philosophers rose yet higher in the city.... Cato determined on some pretext or other to rid and purge the city of them all. So he rose in the Senate...and said: 'We ought to make up our minds one way or another...in order that these men may return to their schools and lecture to the sons of Greece, while the youth of Rome give ear to their laws and magistrates, as heretofore.'

[1] Suet. *De Rhet.* I. [2] Plut. *Cato Maior*, XXII, 5 ff.

[3] Plut. *loc. cit.* XXII. The translation is that of B. Perrin in the Loeb edition.

The fact that this suggestion was complied with shows that a majority of Senators shared Cato's uneasiness. The last sentence gives the clue to the cause of that uneasiness: they wanted the youth of Rome to continue to obey the laws and the magistrates. Obedience to the constituted authority, *disciplina*, was the foundation of the Roman State; their early history was filled with improving stories in illustration of this virtue; the greatness of the Roman army depended on this absolute obedience, and disobedience was sternly punished. The effect of these philosophers on young Romans was to make them question the traditional conceptions of duty, right and wrong, and such questioning appeared to strike at the very roots of the Roman *ethos*, and to demand something more than custom as the basis of society. If such an intellectual ferment were to continue, it seemed to the Senators that the whole of society would be undermined. Athens had put Socrates to death for doing this; the Senate was content to put Rome out of bounds to his successors.

The nobles themselves were perfectly ready to interest themselves in the different schools of philosophy, to discuss the basis of society and the sanctions against wrongdoing, for they knew what they were about; such discussion might mould or influence their views, it would never allow them to call in question the basis of their society, for their position and power were closely connected with its maintenance. Slow change they might admit, but not a revolution. They could not trust the youth and the uneducated to perceive the importance of an established code in a society, which is accepted even by those who do not understand it. They feared—rightly or wrongly, one cannot say—that this questioning was destructive, and would not replace a simpler by a more complex code of society; that what they had would be destroyed, to be replaced by nothing.

They therefore preferred the *mos maiorum*. And it is to this fact that Panaetius owed his great influence upon them. To him Rome was indebted for the philosophical interpretation of her character and aims. His immediate success and subsequent influence were due to his sympathetic approach to the Roman mind and character. Had he come to Rome to show off, he would have found a welcome no warmer than did Carneades. But in his way he was a greater man; by his sympathetic understanding of the Roman character and their ideals he was able to win the confidence of the nobles. He did not seek to dazzle by the brilliance of his logic; he was content to adapt his Stoicism to Roman needs. He took the Roman *ethos* and the aristocratic ideal and gave them a philosophic basis; Stoicism and the ideal became fused in his interpretation. Nothing of the essential elements was changed, nothing was added; the ideal and the *ethos* remained as before, but now they seemed to have a basis in the order of the world, whereas before their only appeal had been to tradition and the *mos maiorum*.

Literature was more easily controlled, for reasons which are not far to seek. The nobles were the educated and leisured class, and from them or from their patronage must come the literature of Rome, since, except for drama, one could not make a living by one's writings; an author, therefore, must either be of independent means, or enjoy the patronage of one who would provide him with a livelihood. Except for history the nobles regarded literature as an accomplishment, not a profession, and would have considered it degrading to publish under their own name anything which did not seem to them worthy of a governor. As patrons they could obviously exercise a complete control of their protégé's work; but this was unnecessary, since they only encouraged those who were in sympathy with their point of view, or were the interpreters of the *ethos* of Roman society without being its critics. Ennius and Terence, therefore, enjoyed the full protection of the Roman nobles; those who might have been antagonistic did not have the opportunity to express themselves.

We must appreciate one important fact; that the educated class at Rome was small, and the book trade primitive. The reading public was therefore small, and was confined in fact to the upper class, who might be ready to read works that seemed critical of established usage or even of themselves, because, as with philosophy, they knew where they stood, and would readily discuss as an academic problem what might with the lower classes have become a live issue. Books did not publicize ideas beyond their own circle. The way to the public was through drama; the stage was the one means of communicating, so to speak, with the Roman people at large. The nobles' attitude towards the written and the spoken word was correspondingly different. The Greek philosophers were chased from Rome for putting novel ideas into the minds of young Romans; but Ennius could write his *Euhemerus* without interference, because the ideas on the nature and origin of the gods would not become the property of persons outside their circle.

Naevius had followed the custom of the Old Attic comedy by criticizing leading personalities and policies, and his boldness met with imprisonment and finally banishment. Such was the beginning and the end of the spirit of old comedy at Rome; free criticism of the governors could only end, as at Athens, with bringing them into contempt and thus bringing disharmony and instability into the State. No succeeding dramatist repeated the experiment. Plautus preferred to restrict his activities to the *fabula palliata*,[1] and even there he was too wise to make Rome the scene of any of his plays. He not merely adapted Greek plays, but was most careful to keep the whole colouring Greek, to leave no doubt that what he was depicting on the stage could not have happened at Rome. The impudent slaves, the dishonest sons, could be laughed at by the Roman audience because they were completely foreign to Rome, and therefore the morals of Rome were not impugned. When comedies in Roman settings began to be written, Donatus tells us[2] that the role of the slave had to be toned down because Roman sentiment would not have tolerated a master being outwitted by his slave. For similar reasons Plautus had to tread carefully in his portrayal of female character; the

[1] A Latin play, based on Greek New Comedy.

[2] Ter. *Eun.* 57.

hetaera (courtesan) could not be shown on the Roman stage as a generous character, since the Roman matrons would have objected; he was therefore compelled to make her an inferior character with little to commend her. In his whole approach we find Plautus accepting the limitations which the governing class imposed on all aspects of public life. Within those limits he could and did work freely; as a professional playwright he could not afford to run counter to the sentiments of the governing class, and his genius succeeded in producing plays which both pleased his audience and satisfied the conditions imposed.

When Titinius came to write *fabulae togatae*[1] he laid the scenes in small Italian towns. It is important that he did not make Rome the scene; Mommsen supposed that the author of *togatae* was obliged to confine his activities to cities with Latin rights, and that the presentation of Rome or of cities with full citizenship was forbidden.[2] Whether it was expressly forbidden we cannot say, nor does it matter; it is sufficient to realize that Rome and cities with full citizenship were not the scenes of comedies. The reason for this is clear, that the nobles, whose anxiety to preserve the Roman *ethos* was so great, would not look with equanimity at plays whose plot revolved around the loose morals of Roman citizens, or in which slaves were called upon to help their masters' sons in some deception at the expense of the *paterfamilias*. Even in the atmosphere of the small Italian towns care must be exercised, since Rome depended on their friendship and support, and their ruling classes were in close alliance with the Roman nobles. It seems that Titinius paid particular attention to his female characters, who would presumably take the place of the Greek *hetaera* for whom the Roman stage had no place. He also toned down the impudence of the slaves, since Roman society kept its slaves, like other classes, in their place.

Greek comedy transplanted to Rome could hardly under these circumstances hope to sustain itself for long. The genius of Plautus

[1] Roman comedies, generally depicting lower life.

[2] *History of Rome* (Eng. trans.), III, 164 and n. 1.

did succeed in imparting to his dramas something of the crude and boisterous spirit which distinguished Rome from Athens. But Terence, the darling of the aristocracy, showed that what was being aimed at was not Roman but Menandrian comedy; and at one remove from the original, written by a man who was not Greek for an audience that preferred the entertainment of the music hall, it was a bloodless shadow of real entertainment for the Roman *plebs*; its elegance of language, care in plot, refinement and absence of crudeness and vulgarity, elicited alike the praise of the educated and the yawns of the people.

Tragedy, too, saw its end during this century, but for different reasons. The spirit of Greek tragedy, its religious brooding and interpretation of human affairs expressed the Greek view of human life and its relations with Heaven. The wrestling with the problem of man's relations with God was not for Roman minds; in this, as in so much else, the Roman felt and accepted, he did not try to express his feelings or to bring the processes of mind to conscious formulation; nor, had he tried to, would his genius have found expression in the form of tragedy.

Rome found its medium for religious interpretation rather in the epic poem, which was Rome's true counterpart to the tragedy of Greece. Rome's destiny, the quality of her character and her men is the theme of her three great epic poems; and this religious epic, with one's country as the central theme, was peculiarly Roman; Greece has nothing to compare with it; and the later religious epics of Dante and Milton, written under different religious convictions, were universal, concerned with the destiny of man, not of a particular nation. In it we see, as in the *praetexta*,[1] the Roman spirit, concerned only with the particular, Rome, and contemplating religion only from that point of view, never posing a universal question or seeking a universal answer.

Thus came to its end this literary form at Rome, imported from without at the nobles' behest, encouraged and in large measure sustained by them during this century, because it seemed to them

[1] A Roman play on a Roman historical theme. See below, p. 40 f.

both good and religious, seemed also not to conflict with the *ethos* of their society. They could not know that it did not properly express themselves or their religious sentiments, because they did not properly at that time understand themselves; it flourished at their behest, it died in spite of them, because the soil was alien. It is true that with their blessing there had come to being their own true form of religious expression, the epic; but one may wonder whether tragedy would have been cultivated at all at Rome, had not the Romans found themselves suddenly confronted with the literature of Greece at a time when one class could impose its wishes and its tastes on all. Their control of literature is seen no less in what they allowed than in what they forbade.

These examples from the three realms of religion, philosophy and literature illustrate the attitude of the nobles towards their society. The examples could be multiplied, and examples from other spheres such as education could be given to confirm the general impression. We see a close-knit, closely integrated society, divided into classes, each with its own sphere of interests and activities, and all acknowledging and respecting the rights and activities of the others. It was an aristocratic society, in which the nobles, with general assent, sustained all the burdens and responsibilities of government, receiving in return fame, position and influence. It was a harmonious society, in which the claims of the city-state, Rome, held a supreme place; if there was among any group a feeling of discontent, it never went so far as to endanger the State; discontent had to find its satisfaction within prescribed and generally accepted limits. It was a society that believed in its future, felt that it was different and better than others, and was certain that this superiority was the result of its past and the greatness of its ancestors, and that Rome was under the special care of Heaven. The nobles, therefore, showed a great concern to maintain the purity of their social code from outside taints; their instinct told them that a stable society must have deep roots, and that many of the customs and practices of a society lose their original significance, to acquire a second, spiritual meaning, whose understanding is not susceptible to reason but only to the spirit of a member of that society. It was in consequence a happy society, conservative though it was; changes came, but they came slowly and had the support of most men in consequence; societies evolve and change; for the society of Rome to remain aristocratic would in any case have been impossible, and its passage from aristocracy to some more broad form of society could have come to pass; Fate decreed that it should move from aristocracy through revolution to autocracy; and the Gracchi were Fate's instruments.

CHAPTER IV

NAEVIUS, ENNIUS AND ROMAN EPIC

We may with advantage consider here certain aspects of the two great epic poems of this period, for from them we may be able to distil something of the qualities of the Roman character and of the Roman attitude towards Rome and Heaven, which for a true understanding of this period are essential. Too often Roman literature is criticized against the glittering background of Greece, and any slight brilliance it may seem to radiate is at once shown to be but a reflection of something far more brilliant in that background. It is true that Fate ordained that Rome should look to Greece for form and style, and on occasion for inspiration also; but Rome had none the less her own soul, and she found means to express it, even though she might use the mould of Greece. We shall here attempt merely to extract from these poems certain qualities whose recognition will guide us to an understanding of certain important aspects of the Roman character, and this understanding will in its turn, perhaps, throw light on the underlying motives and values of the men who fashioned the destinies of Rome during this period.

We may turn first to Naevius. He wrote his epic on the first Punic War during the second Punic War. Why he chose the more distant war we cannot say for certain; he had taken part in it, and that may perhaps have had some slight influence; but in itself it can be but a trifling reason. He was a witness of the second war, and his greater age would have revealed those deeper aspects which must have remained veiled from the eyes of youth. But to the artist that very nearness could have been a drawback; the clash of group and policy became insistent during the later years, involving finally himself; the message of the poem might have been lost amid the quarrels of those to whom he had not given enough of praise and honour. And when he began his work, the war was not yet ended; that is important; he chose to write of the clash between Rome and Carthage while yet Carthage was unbeaten. We must imagine the poet in the atmosphere of stress and strain of the Hannibalic War, when it must still after many years of fighting be uncertain whether Rome would defeat Hannibal; we must imagine the poet in his sensitivity seeing the struggle as something deeper than a fight between two jungle beasts, and deciding to interpret for his countrymen that deeper meaning which gave sense to their struggle and their sorrows. For the artist it mattered not which war he took; and since he wished to show the meaning of the present, uncompleted war, it was perhaps natural to turn to the first war, where perspective was clearer and present passions not involved, in order to explain the struggle between Rome and Carthage.

I have inferred from the circumstances of its composition and from its theme that Naevius had some purpose other than to compile a dull chronicle of the first war, and I have suggested that this purpose was to show the clash of Rome and Carthage as being something more than a mere fight between the lion and the tiger; to fit it, in fact, into a Roman pattern and give it a Roman meaning, thus to inspire and fortify his struggling countrymen. Let us look more closely at the poem. We know that Naevius treated of Rome's foundation, beginning with Aeneas' escape from Troy and giving attention to his meeting with Dido. At first sight we might ask why he should have given so much time and space (nearly three books out of seven) to Rome's foundation; there must have been some compelling reason, especially when we remember that nothing else in Rome's past history was touched upon. It could certainly provide a cause for the Punic Wars, a cause that would go back even before Rome's first beginnings; but only on one condition, namely that it was acceptable to Romans on those terms. Unless Rome's cast of mind and attitude were such that they could believe in such a cause, it was foolish, if not tasteless, to waste three books on an irrelevant fairy story.

We may now proceed a little further. Macrobius, referring to Jupiter's great speech in Book I of the *Aeneid*, comments thus:

> In principio Aeneidos tempestas describitur et Venus apud Iovem queritur;...hic locus totus sumptus a Naevio est ex primo libro Punici belli. Illic enim aeque Venus Troianis tempestate laborantibus cum Iove queritur, et secuntur verba Iovis filiam consolantis spe futurorum.[1]

We are familiar with Jupiter's speech in Virgil, its great importance for understanding Virgil's conception of Rome, and its promise of Rome's future greatness. This will perhaps help us to understand the significance of Naevius' inclusion of Rome's foundation. It connected Rome with Heaven, and made its foundation and history Heaven's special care; as in Virgil, Rome's destiny was written centuries before her foundation; that destiny would not be easy, but it was assured; Jupiter unrolls the great *spes futurorum* at a moment of great peril to Aeneas, a peril that was to bring into being Carthage's undying hatred of the unborn city; and it is precisely at the genesis of that hatred that Jupiter gives Rome her reassurance. This is not accident, it is the design of the poet; just when the Romans were fighting for their lives against the Punic foe, Naevius shows them that the struggle was part of Rome's destiny, that it was inescapable, yet that it was her destiny to emerge and, once the monster was subdued, to continue on her fated course. That was the *spes futurorum* with which Jupiter consoled Venus in her anguish, the *spes* also which Naevius gives his readers; Rome's destiny was difficult but assured; and it was Heaven's ordinance.

This is the importance for our purpose of Rome's foundation in the poem, provided—and only provided—it would chime with Roman sentiment. If it would seem to them nothing but conventional divine machinery,* then it would be stupid and tasteless to include it here; for of one thing we may be sure; the poem sprang from the deep emotions of the time. One feels too deeply in the midst of war to be content with Hellenistic gods; and if Naevius

[1] Macrobius, VI, 2, 31.

included Jupiter and Aeneas' travels, it was because he felt that he could say through them something of what his countrymen were feeling inchoately.

We may note one thing more in connexion with Rome's foundation in Naevius. It was long supposed that Naevius first described the foundation, and then proceeded immediately to the first Punic War. This created difficulties, but resourceful emending scholars had little difficulty in compelling the fragments to conform to this simple scheme, thus leaving to Naevius, to say the least, a crudity in treatment. But a modern scholar[1] has at once shown that the ancients were not in need of the emender's art, and that Naevius was a greater poet than they had dared suppose. The poem began, not with Rome's foundation, but with the first Punic War, continuing down to the fall of Agrigentum in 262 B.C. At that point Naevius turned aside to describe the great temple of Zeus, on whose west pediment was depicted the fall of Troy, and thus led into the story of Aeneas' flight and Rome's foundation. This is artistically fine; it is also significant for our purpose. It gave a religious opening for the story of the foundation, and gave it a religious setting, the pediment of the temple of Zeus, i.e. to Roman sentiment, of Jupiter, Rome's own god, the god who has laid down for her Rome's destiny.

The religious quality of the poem thus becomes clear, and raises it to a level which the wretched fragments would withhold from it; it gives Naevius a place among the poets, not the versifiers, of Rome, her first great epic poet, portraying the struggle between Rome and Carthage as a struggle ordained by destiny, from which Rome was to emerge triumphant. We can see also that for his purpose the first war was better than the second; the uncertainty of the present was turned to assurance through the poet's interpretation of the first.

We may now turn to Ennius' poem. It embraced the whole

[1] L. Strzelecki, *De Naeviano Belli Punici carmine quaestiones selectae.* See Marmorale, *Naevius Poeta* (2nd ed. 1950), 29 ff., 174 ff.; Rostagni, *Letteratura Latina*, I, 102 n. 3, 103, 110. See now Fraenbel in *J.R.S.* XLIV (1954), 14 ff.

history of Rome from its foundation down to his own time, though it touched only slightly on the first Punic War, which had been treated by Naevius. Time, though it has not been lavish, has been kinder in preserving precious fragments than it has with Naevius, and few and tantalizing though they are, there are enough to show the religious quality of the poem. Throughout the fragments are to be found lines and passages of deep and moving quality, charged with the religious tones of one who felt and believed in his theme; lines also which show us those qualities of character which the Romans believed to be theirs, a part of their divine legacy as Heaven's chosen instruments. It is not the mere divine machinery of epic; so far as we can see, the gods did not take active part in Rome's battles; the idea of presenting the gods in Heaven was suggested to him by epic practice, but he has turned the practice, as did Naevius, to his own purpose, and has reserved the occasions of their appearance for a special use. They seem not to have intermingled with men as in the simpler days of Homer or the uncomprehending days of the Empire; only, as in Naevius, do they seem perhaps directly to have concerned themselves in the days of Aeneas' wanderings; at other times they remain apart, in their Olympian abode, concerned to see Rome's progress, but neither interfering nor intervening.

The account of Romulus and Remus watching for the omen that was to decide who should found the new city[1] shows the deep, religious quality of his poetry, and the sincerity of his belief in Rome's foundation by the gods; and that same deep, religious quality is shown in the magnificent lines in which the Romans lament the death of Romulus, lines which we may quote, because they emphasize the close relationship of Rome with the gods:[2]

O Romule, Romule die,
Qualem te patriae custodem di genuerunt!
O pater, O genitor, O sanguen dis oriundum,
Tu produxisti nos intra luminis oras.

[1] Vahlens3, 77–96; Warmington, *Remains of Old Latin*, I, 80–100.
[2] Vahlens, 110–14; Warmington, 117–21.

The connexion between Heaven and Rome could not be closer; in each of the first three lines it is emphasized; Romulus is born to be the guardian of Rome; just as the 'di genuerunt Romulum', so is Romulus the 'genitor' of Rome. Romulus is the gods' instrument for founding Rome, and to Heaven he returns his mission once accomplished.

This religious strain runs through many of the fragments, and indicates what must have been the tone of the work. But there was no boastfulness; one of the finest speeches we possess is spoken, not by a Roman, but by Pyrrhus;[1] if Rome defeated Pyrrhus, it was not good defeating evil, for Pyrrhus, too, was honourable; it was part of Rome's destiny, because in order to contend with Carthage she must first defeat Pyrrhus. There is a note in Servius on l. 20, Bk. I of the *Aeneid*: 'in Ennio inducitur Iuppiter promittens Romanis excidium Carthaginis'. Here, as in Naevius, and later in Virgil, we have a scene in Heaven in which Rome's destiny is set forth by Jupiter himself, a destiny which culminates in the defeat of the most dangerous enemy Rome ever knew; his readers, newly emerged from that great struggle, would feel their destiny, feel further that they as Romans must be the actors in this great drama whose plot Jove himself had written.

He dealt but slightly with the first Punic War, because Naevius had, in rough, unpolished verse, already sung it. Yet if Naevius' poem had not treated it in a way conformable to his own treatment of Roman history, he would have dealt fully with that war too; its importance was too great to be omitted from the scheme of Roman history. But he was able to pass it over just because Naevius' treatment corresponded with his own handling of the rest of Roman history; they were both giving the same interpretation to their countrymen, and therefore he could pass it by in silence.

By the age of Augustus Rome's destiny had become clear;[2] in

[1] Vahlens, 194–201; Warmington, 186–93.

[2] It found its expression in the *Aeneid*, with which it is not possible to deal here.

the second century it was still but dimly felt, nor indeed could it have been otherwise. Since there is no earlier Latin literature, we cannot know for certain whether that feeling came to birth in the second Punic War, or whether it was there before. But at least it could only have come to birth if the Roman cast of mind and religious attitude allowed of such a genesis; it must have been conformable to their beliefs, from which alone it could have sprung. It has been pointed out[1] that much in Rome's own tradition of her past shows an aloofness, a separateness from other people; the original inhabitants were castaways from other societies, and criminals, their first brides were snatched from the Sabines; later, they emphasized their Trojan descent, which made them aliens to Italy; and, in spite of their racial kinship, they were reluctant to admit the Latins as of their kin. All this reveals a feeling of difference from their neighbours; and that feeling must have grown to greater keenness in the centuries that followed, as Rome came gradually to dominate the whole peninsula. Similarly the idea of their close connexion with Heaven is perhaps shown in the triumphal ceremony, wherein the victorious general's face was smeared to personate Jupiter himself; at that moment the general was not Jove's agent, but Jove himself. We may note, too, the religious character of their declaration of war, which shows the Romans as feeling in those early days that the war they were embarking on was not of their making but their enemy's, that their action had their gods' approval, and that their gods were concerned for the welfare of their city.

If, as I believe, that feeling was already there, the wars against Carthage must have sharpened it; in two great struggles with a mighty state, whose vast reserves of wealth made those of Rome contemptible, a state whose skill at sea was great, whose fighting qualities had won her empire, and whose money could buy her the best of mercenaries, none the less she had through dogged perseverance and faith in herself succeeded in turning aside and

[1] See Altheim, *History of Roman Religion* (Eng. trans.), 411 ff.; *Röm. Gesch.* I, 203 ff.

finally destroying this Minotaur of the western sea. She had had nothing but her qualities of character and her men to match against the wealth and skill of Carthage: 'moribus antiquis stat res Romana virisque'. Romans on the morrow of Zama cannot have been insensitive to the meaning of that day, which Jupiter had promised them close on a thousand years ago.

But if that feeling was sharpened by this experience, Rome's history had still further to unroll itself before her destiny could be distinctly seen; in Ennius (and almost certainly in Naevius) they were content to feel that they were playing a part in Heaven's drama, and that their performance depended on their qualities of character and their moral code, their *virtus*. That feeling of destiny was lost in the period of disintegration of the first century; Cicero seeks unsuccessfully to remind Romans of themselves, Sallust knows that Rome has fallen from herself; Varro tries to restore Rome's *prisca virtus*; but all to no avail in that unhappy age of failure and surrender from her great ideals. It was not until the age of Augustus, when the Roman world emerged at last from the carnage and the degradation of its civil war, that Romans, ashamed of what had been, found their souls once more in the peace which followed Actium, and recognized their destiny. And Virgil was its poet. By now it could be seen, not merely felt; as they looked upon the bitter past, they saw how they had failed themselves and the Empire which they held in trust; and Virgil set before his countrymen the Roman ideal, in lines which will be ever memorable;[1] nothing selfish, boastful or grandiose, but Heaven's mission to civilize the world.

Three points emerge from this brief survey of the poems, their religious quality, their central theme of Rome, and their sense of destiny and of Rome's close association with Heaven. We may take these points and pursue them a little further, for they are not accidental, but spring from the depths of the Roman character, and go far to explain her success and limitations, not merely at this time but throughout her history.

[1] *Aeneid*, VI, 847 ff.

When Rome's political and military success brought her into direct contact with Greek literature and thought, her own literature had developed but little; there was nothing which she could set beside the supreme achievements of Greece. It was therefore natural and necessary that in a world where she was becoming steadily more important, she should be affected by that world's higher culture both in literature and art. It was in some ways unfortunate that this should be so; her own literature did not have the chance to develop along its own lines, to produce its own forms which should reflect and express the people whose literature it was. To continue with the slow development of native forms and native verses became impossible when Greece's polished products were in her hands; and Roman literature suffered to some extent from this unfortunate circumstance. Yet Rome made no surrender; the robust independence of the Roman character showed itself here no less than in the realm of politics.

One of the Greek forms of literature which early came to Rome was the tragic drama, which was written in Rome for rather more than a century. But it failed to sustain itself at Rome; by the first century tragedy and comedy had ceased to be written; the great writers of the second century came to be regarded as 'classics', but as a living form it had ceased, to become the sport of dilettante writers, its place taken by the more indigenous dramatic forms of the mime and the Atellane farce, in which the cruder Roman character found greater pleasure.

The reason for its failure, not far to seek, is instructive. Tragedy was a peculiarly Greek form, developed from its crudest beginnings to its final perfection without adulteration from outside, for the expression of the feelings and the attitude of the Greeks towards Heaven. In its finished form it was suited to the handling of the problems of man's relations to God as the Greek mind perceived those problems; both form and problem were Greek, as were the great dramatists, Aeschylus and Sophocles. The form presupposed a certain attitude and outlook on the part of writer and audience; it could only therefore hope to flourish in

Rome if the Roman attitude and outlook were similar to those in Greece.

But in this matter Rome and Greece were utterly opposed; to the Greek the problems of religion were universal. Aeschylus is concerned with the relation of God to man, not of Zeus to the Athenians, the reason for man's suffering, not his own. Sophocles shows how man must suffer, even though he be not wicked; Euripides is concerned with the unworthy stories and motives attributed to God; while Aristotle emphasizes the universal as a first necessity of tragedy. Themistocles is nowhere mentioned in the *Persae*; the problem is a universal one, how a few had defeated a great empire, and the answer lay in Heaven and its immutable laws; the few had obeyed those laws, the Persians had set themselves in defiance of them, and Zeus' punishment had followed. In religion, as in so much else, Greece gave the world one of its greatest legacies, the universal; her greatest contributions, as her greatest failures, are in no small measure due to this quality of her mind.

The Roman genius was wholly different; the universal was foreign to their nature; always the 'this' and the 'that'. Roman literature has nothing to set beside Greek tragedy and philosophy from this point of view; not until Christianity gave a universality transcending men and race does such appear in the Latin tongue. When they imported Greek tragedy, they imported a product alien to their spirit. They could not understand as a Greek could the problems that were in question, nor would they have felt that they were important or even relevant to them; their thoughts ran on different lines. Since the initial interest was lacking, no one attempted to adapt it to their needs (with one exception); it was alien, and could never win to Roman citizenship. They merely put Greek tragedies on the Roman stage; for a time it satisfied, while the newly created interest in things Greek continued, and while there was no substitute; but it could not survive when the Roman genius had grown to consciousness.

One modification they did attempt to tragedy, the *praetexta*, and it is significant, for it shows us one of those traits which are the key to the understanding of their outlook and their character. In the *praetexta* an episode of Roman history formed the plot, and the Romans who had taken the leading part in the events became the central characters in the play. Let us first observe the difference between this treatment of a Roman historical theme and Aeschylus' treatment in the *Persae*; the Greek universal, the Roman particular, the Greek deliberately omitting, the Roman concerned to stress, the individual. Since we have no surviving *praetexta* of this century, we cannot say with certainty how the theme was treated; we may, however, suppose that Rome was shown surmounting its crisis with the help of those who took their part, and also probably of Heaven; for we cannot be certain how the gods were handled. The *praetexta* could lend itself to abuse, to the lauding of some family; but it shows us the Roman character in its distinction from the Greek, concerned only with the particular, Rome, and with the individual, seeing its religion through Rome and the individual, never seeking to go beyond those limits, contracting the Greek universal within those limits.

This particularity is one of the outstanding Roman characteristics, a particularity identified with Rome, which acquires—or, it may be, gives—in consequence a religious quality. Rome was their all, made universal by being the religious centre-point; but the universal was none the less still Rome and Roman; it could only become universal in practice when all the world was Rome. Throughout her history Rome sought rather to make Roman, until her constant expansion found its completion when Rome was all the world. She never worked from *a priori* theories of universality or equality, as did Greece; she worked instinctively, and made things Roman. Only when she realized that much of the world was Roman, did she try to provide the theory; and generally her reason failed to understand her instinct; but in those attempts to give the theory we see the deeply held assumption that to make Roman was a blessing to mankind, and a duty for Rome herself.

Eternal Rome was the central point of a Roman's religious awe;

it followed that Rome must be the central theme of any religious poem which sought to express the religious convictions of Romans. Theirs was not the imagination to show eternal truth through fable; all they could do was to try to communicate their belief in Rome's destiny by showing it in action; their religious views must be expressed in terms both of Rome and of reality, and the expression must therefore take the form of an account of Rome in history. Since they conceived of Rome and themselves as actually working out Rome's destiny, the poem must be factual, or based on facts; the poet's task was to make clear Heaven's purpose, and Rome's central place in the evolution of that purpose; Rome's actual history must be shown to be an essential part of that process, which was still continuing and would continue until the purpose had been attained. In Naevius and Ennius the final purpose was not yet clearly seen; the Romans must go forward in faith, if not in understanding, clear only of a mission and an attendant responsibility. By Virgil's time the vision was clear, and the Romans could continue on their civilizing mission, knowing now the burden and the road.

The Roman religious instinct therefore found its own unique form of expression, an epic poem dealing with Rome and her destiny, based on the facts of Roman history. To regard them as anything but religious poems is to misunderstand them as much as one would a Greek tragedy, if one regarded it in terms of the modern drama. They were the religious expression of a society at a certain point of its development, and Virgil was the last true such poet. It is perhaps not without significance that Lucan excluded Heaven to substitute the Stoic Fatum; Virgil married them, and thus gave Fatum a positive quality; Lucan divorced them and made of Fatum an inescapable necessity against which it was vain to fight, even though to fight were noble. Both were the products of their time, and we may sympathize with Lucan's sense of powerlessness to change a destiny he would be glad to alter; like others of his contemporaries he saw only the negative, oppressive side of Zeno's Fatum, which forced men to live in tyranny, and allowed them no escape but suicide. Virgil and the Augustans saw its positive side, buoyant and encouraging, giving men justification to do what they wanted to do, filling them with a sense of humble pride and responsibility at being partners in the realization of Heaven's purpose: 'ducunt volentem Fata, nolentem trahunt'.

This insistence on Rome meets us equally in their historians. Rome is the centre for almost all Roman historians, great and small; the universal histories were not written in the Latin tongue, only Roman histories. Livy did for Roman history what Virgil did for its epic, made it universal by equating Rome with the universal. Sallust, though anxious to see through Thucydides' eyes, could not escape from Rome and the particular to see the particular as a phenomenon of human society; it was a phenomenon of first-century Roman society, not as in Thucydides, a phenomenon of human society under certain strains and circumstances. It is to this refusal to generalize and to this steadfast concentration on Rome that her success in law and politics is largely due; and no one who fails to mark them will rightly understand the reasons both for her successes and her failures.

The epic poets of the Empire did not have these qualities; they did not, because they could not, follow Rome's own epic tradition; what Statius and Flaccus wrote belongs rather to the dead heap of Hellenistic research, reflecting and expressing nothing of their society beyond its soulless education. Silius tried to revive Rome's own tradition, but revived only the dead ghost, whose vital spirit, when it had lived, he did not understand; the Punic War, with all the trappings of the divine machinery and the exaggerations of the schools of rhetoric, makes but a poor and feeble fourth beside the great trinity. Lucan is better; but the circumstances of Empire have changed the outlook; he is Roman, but a disgruntled one; he has something of the qualities we have noted in the earlier poets, but they have all been warped; the note of hope and confidence has become the wailing of frustration, and the destiny he sees he fears.

But in these other poets we see the unique product of the Roman genius, their own expression of their own religious faith, as tragedy was of Greece. We see moreover some of those qualities and limitations which helped to make the Romans what they were; when we say that the Romans produced no philosophy, we should remember that the reasons for that failure were also the reasons for her ecumenical empire; that the limitations—if limitations they be—of their thought were imposed upon them by that selfsame particularity and aversion from the universal which enabled them to go slowly forward, enlarging, as it were, the *pomerium* until it girdled the earth; and that had they accepted all that Greece had to offer, the gift must have destroyed that quality of insularity which made possible the Roman Empire. The universals of Greece were valuable to Rome because she fitted them to her own conception, and was thus able to identify the universal with her own concept, Rome. Concentration on Rome and a belief in her Heaven-imposed destiny, these were Roman and Roman epic.

PART II

THE CONSEQUENCES OF VICTORY

CHAPTER V

FOREIGN POLICY

Rome was now the most important city of Italy, with which Latium and the rest of Italy were joined in a diverse system of alliances. This was the outcome of centuries of struggle, through which had slowly emerged by trial and experimentation this organization, an organization which had proved equally fruitful to Rome and to the constituent members. Rome and her allies had defeated the Carthaginians in one war, and in the aftermath had become possessed of the islands of Sardinia and Corsica as well as Sicily; in 200 B.C. she had just emerged from the death-struggle of the second Punic War, a war which had tested to the limit every link in the chain of her confederation, and in which very few of the links had proved weak. The weak ones had been strengthened; Rome and her confederation could gaze with awe upon the huge giant which now lay at her feet, and which, in spite of the mortal terror it had at first created, in spite of the vast damage it had wrought throughout the length and breadth of Italy, now panted prostrate, awaiting the signal of the victor's thumb.

Rome had fought for her very existence; not surprisingly therefore in the treaty of peace she took stringent precautions against the resurgence of the military might of Carthage. Her commerce was left free; but her military strength was strictly confined. This was natural; Rome's position was not yet assured; her important wars had been fought in self-defence or to prevent others becoming strong enough to constitute a menace; and to her the Mediterranean world with its Hellenistic monarchies was an arena in which others could rise to threaten her security or existence.

Her experience with Carthage had made it clear to her that, as armies might march into Italy from the West, so they might from the East,* and that as a seaborne army could be taken to and from Carthage and Italy, so could armies sail from Greece. The neutralizing of Greece was therefore her first concern. From the West she was secure; she must establish a similar security from the East. She did not want to possess Greece, nor did she feel towards her the responsibilities of a guardian; she merely wished to keep it free of any strong external state. The maintenance of Greece as a neutral zone, with her 'independence' guaranteed by Rome alone was the cardinal point of Rome's policy during these years. Fears that it might be occupied by Philip V, Antiochus the Great and Perseus were chiefly responsible for her three major wars. She was determined to allow no strategic disadvantage to develop, and since Greece in the wrong hands seemed to present just that disadvantage, there arose what we may call this 'preventive habit', which continued, as we shall see, when changed circumstances no longer required this precaution. The use she made of her victories acquits her of imperialistic designs or ruthless power-politics. The first two wars added not one acre of territory to her possessions; having contained these princes within their domains and having thus freed Greece from their activities, she left them free to pursue their ambitions where they would not worry Rome. Even when Macedon's independence ended, Rome made no effort to exploit the country; at first it was divided into four Republics, paying to Rome but half the tribute they had paid their king; and only with reluctance did Rome assume direct responsibility for its government, when it would not be peaceable, and hence became a source of worry.

Her attitude to and treatment of Greece itself well illustrate the limitations of Rome's outlook, which are to be discerned in all her foreign policy, and which were the result of her political immaturity. While Greece was wholly within Rome's orbit, Rome was content; Greece could live whatever life she chose, within her own confines combine in whatever system of leagues and alliances she pleased.* Further, Rome wanted her to do that; she did not want, and never contemplated, the assumption of any responsibility for Greece's government, or her economic and social progress. Her interest was narrowly political, concerned only with Rome's security. Yet it was impossible to confine her interests within so narrow a compass; Rome's very shadow across their country displeased many Greeks; their social and economic problems were great, and it was not surprising that later on many Greeks, displeased that Rome interfered in their internal affairs without solving their internal problems, turned to outside help.

The natural consequence was further Roman interference, and thus relations continued to be bedevilled between the two countries. Greece was in fact not free, yet Rome wanted her to act as though she were, although to do so might well provoke Rome's anger. Rome could not see Greece's dilemma, because she was thinking only in terms of her own safety, and knew little of Greece's internal problems beyond the point where they ceased to affect Rome's safety. She did not see that social and economic conditions affected politics, and her own interest was strictly political; hence she could not see that she was denying Greece the right to live her own life, while refusing to organize it for her.

Yet we should not convict her of wilful irresponsibility. It was the behaviour of a State whose chief concern was her own safety, at a time when she could not take her safety for granted; of a State that had no overseas ambitions, and was herself conscious of no moral responsibilities outside herself. It is unjust to criticize Rome for that; it is a phase through which all States pass during their growth and development; and the fair question is whether within the limits of her development she behaved with moderation and a sense of responsibility. Her refusal to extend her territory proves both her moderation* and also her city-state mentality, her patience with the Greeks, whose problems she did not understand, and whom she therefore came to despise for not behaving like Romans, was considerable. She tried hard to make a contented Greece and could not understand the reason for her failure; it was only after fifty years of sincere effort that her patience broke down.

Her policy towards more distant States followed the same pattern of guarding her security without involving herself in responsibility for the welfare of the States. Since her safety was only remotely involved at the periphery, her policy consisted in the maintenance of a balance of power between the important States, and a complete lack of interest otherwise. We need not examine the details of her interference and advice in the East; in her dealings with Pergamum and Egypt the checking of Syria's power was her main aim, and beyond the maintenance of a balance of power she did not aspire to go. It was a frontier policy, such as the emperors pursued with Armenia and Parthia, and the British in many parts of the world.

By her defeat of Carthage Rome had become one of the powerful States of the Mediterranean world, but certainly not the most powerful; and, more important, was not conscious that she had entered the ranks of the powerful States. She might look upon her achievement with something of the awe with which the Athenians regarded Marathon; but she could not see that Zama had put her in a posture to stand as an equal beside the powerful Hellenistic monarchies. Situations may change in a day; but it often takes decades to discover the fact.

Rome was now in fact a powerful State, and with the passing of the years she grew more powerful in comparison with the other States. But there was no change in her mental outlook to correspond with her changed position. She was still, as she always had been, apprehensive of powers that might seem to present a threat to her safety; and this attitude of self-defensive apprehension characterizes her foreign policy throughout this period. Her mental outlook continued that of the city-state, whose sphere of responsibility was confined to its own interests, its self-preservation and the provision of what was necessary for that purpose. There is a great difference between a powerful State—which Rome was—and what I may call a 'world-power'—which Rome was not—a difference not merely of relation to other States but of mental outlook and conception of moral responsibility. When a

State has reached that point where she is incontestably the strongest power, with whom none singly within her sphere may hope to join issue, as Rome in Imperial times, England in the later nineteenth century, the U.S.A. today, I call such States 'world-powers'. In such circumstances the State may abandon its traditional attitude of self-defence and apprehension, and awaken to a sense of responsibility towards the weaker States who must look to her for help, or she may rejoice to have no further obstacle to the exploitation of her strength, which none can now prevent.* This change from the outlook of a powerful State to that of a 'world-power' may come as the result of a gradual realization of her new position, as it did with England, or as the result of violent convulsions within the State or the system of which that State is a part, as happened in Rome and the U.S.A.* But there will necessarily be a political time-lag between the time at which all the material conditions of a 'world-power' were satisfied and the realization of that fact by the State. There will be a period of which it will be possible in retrospect to say that the policy of the State was governed by considerations of self-defence, though there was nothing to fear, when she should more properly have been concerned with her responsibilities towards others. In 200 B.C. Rome was a powerful State; by 146 B.C. she was ready to be a 'world-power', but did not realize it. That realization was frustrated for a century by the Gracchi, nor did it come until the Pax Augusta, which put an end to a century's civil discord.*

We must, therefore, consider Rome's foreign policy from this point of view, from which alone we are justified in considering it; it is wrong to apply canons of criticism to her behaviour which are applicable to a State indisputably the strongest in her world, and aware of some at least of the attendant responsibilities. It is as a powerful State, with the organization and mentality of a city-state, that she must be criticized, and her success or failure, her consciousness of moral obligations must be measured by this standard.

We may take three incidents which illustrate the limitation—if it is proper to call limitation what is more truly lack of development—in Rome's outlook during these years, the destruction of Corinth, of Carthage, and her treatment of Rhodes. At first sight the destruction of Corinth seems an act of wanton and irresponsible behaviour by a strong State towards a city that, however provoking, could never deserve such a fate. But Rome had not yet consciously calculated her strength in comparison with the rest of the world, and hence had not appreciated the implications of her superior strength; her reactions towards the outside world were the same as they had been at the beginning of the century. It was still axiomatic that Greece must be a Roman protectorate, even though, had she but thought, there was now no strong power to occupy it. She still felt no responsibility towards Greece, and still expected Greece to run her own affairs 'freely', yet without causing trouble for Rome. When the Achaean League became—to Rome, incomprehensibly—thoroughly disgruntled and actually made war on Rome, patience snapped, the 'independence' which the Greeks perversely refused to enjoy was taken from them, and Rome resigned herself to administering the country which stubbornly refused to run itself.

The sack of Corinth, a city rich in history and in the possession of artistic treasures, seemed to the ancient world a terrible thing.* Yet to the Roman mind it was the punishment meted out by an angry victor as a warning; just as Carthage, Numantia, and Fregellae would suffer, and as Plataea and Thebes had suffered at the hands of the Greeks themselves in the days of their greatness.* Rome behaved at this moment as a strong power that was governed by all the considerations that had shaped her policy for fifty years, and while the rest of the world could see Rome's overwhelming power and hence the needlessness of the act, Rome could not see herself as others saw her. Its effect on the contemporary world was great, because they feared what this mammoth might do next; she might turn to ruthless conquest, which might engulf them. In fact, the history of the previous fifty years had shown, had they been in a position to see, that this would not be; it was one of her last preventive acts, a reflex action made at a time when it had become superfluous; hence both their disquiet and the needlessness for that disquiet.

The destruction of Carthage in the same year illustrates even more clearly this critical moment in Rome's political and moral development. The name of Carthage could arouse quite irrational fears in the breasts of the Romans; there were still alive a few who had lived through the Hannibalic War, and to all of them the story of the terrible fight, the defeats, the near-disaster was a source of fear, should it recur. They had consistently supported Massinissa against Carthage,* the unknown against the known, and while none of Massinissa's actions roused their fear, anything that Carthage attempted provoked immediate retaliation. They could not see the situation in perspective; their thoughts and reactions were those of Rome the city-state, who must be on her guard to prevent the growth of any State able to threaten her security;* and the very name of Carthage was too wrapped about with fearful memories to make reason and tolerance easy. Hence they behaved dishonourably, and were not content until they had removed their fear by razing the supposed threat and scattering its inhabitants.

Particularly instructive as an indication of the political theory and the psychology that lay behind it is the reason given by Scipio Nasica for allowing Carthage to continue: in order that there should be some State of whom Rome stood in awe.[1] Here we see the enunciation of the political thought which had directed Rome's policy during these years, the ultimate position of the preventive, self-defensive attitude. It is the proof that the Romans had not woken up to the responsibilities of a 'world-power', that they were not yet aware that they were one. Scipio could see only that if Rome were wholly safe, if in fact she were to achieve what her foreign policy for fifty years had set out to achieve, then the Romans might start behaving irresponsibly, and her self-discipline might be corrupted. The attitude of Scipio Aemilianus, on the

[1] Diodorus, XXXIV, 33, 4 ff.; Plutarch, *Cato*, XXVII, 2 ff.

other hand, who approved its utter destruction,[1] was the logical consequence of that policy; if her aim was to guard her security, then it was best guarded by destroying all possible opponents.

This was the critical moment in the story of Rome's growth to world dominion. It was symbolized by the unnecessary destruction of these two cities in pursuance of a policy which had directed her actions for generations, and had now become out of date. She had seemingly nothing more to do; she had attained her object; what, then, next? Well might the world wait expectantly to see the direction of her next step, for the world lay at Rome's mercy.

The consummation of their lifetime's policy left the minds of Rome's leaders temporarily without direction. There was a relaxation of tension, now that they had achieved their aim, before some fresh ideal was set before them, and that relaxation showed itself in many spheres; the protraction of the Spanish War, marked as it was by incompetence and dishonesty, by lack of discipline in the army, was one sign of it; now began that deterioration in standards of honesty and propriety which Polybius notes,[2] and which we know from Lucilius to have been a source of concern to Scipio's circle. But such a temporary relaxation was natural, if unfortunate; the important point is that it was far from universal, and that the better men were worried by its manifestation. The solution could consist only in the creation of some ideal of policy to replace the one that had been achieved, and must take the form of some *ratio imperii*. Had their minds not been temporarily devoid of policy, it is unlikely that the Gracchi could have had so profound an effect.

The problem was great, far greater than most modern historians are prepared to concede; it was nothing less than the problem of emerging from the mentality and organization of a city-state to become the capital of an Empire, with a sense of moral responsibility not only to her own provinces but to the rest of the world. The days when Rome could think only of herself were past, and

[1] See Gelzer, *Philologus*, XL (1931), 288–9 = *Vom Röm. Staat*, I, 111 ff.

[2] XVIII, 35; XXXI, 25, 3 ff.

a complete reorientation was necessary for her new role; Stoic philosophers, seeing the problem from outside, might help, but only Romans could do it. Theirs was the problem to prepare for the future without destroying the past, and such reform can come only from within. Only a Roman could know how to change Rome's city-state institutions without uprooting society in the process.

Her changing relations and treatment of Rhodes illustrate a similar tendency in her policy during these years. Rhodes was a strong and important member of the Mediterranean community in 200 B.C., and for some years, while her policy led her to help Rome, she was rewarded, listened to with respect and held in high esteem. But Rhodes, able to observe impartially the gradually changing Mediterranean situation, began to realize that Rome in the process of protecting herself from her supposed enemies was herself becoming very powerful and a source of anxiety to other States. Rhodes realized that she must depend for a continuance of her position and influence on a balance of power between the great States, of which she numbered Rome one, and she was consequently not wholly favourable to Rome in the third Macedonian War. She perceived that the complete defeat of Perseus would leave Rome unpleasantly the strongest State, against which it would be idle for Rhodes to match her strength. Her sympathies, therefore, like those of several others, were with Perseus. The smaller Mediterranean States were beginning to be uneasy at Rome's growth, and to feel that a strong Macedon was a guarantee against Roman tyranny.

Rome won and Rhodes suffered. Saved from war by the sympathetic and forthright speaking of Cato, she was punished and in the event reduced to economic impotence. We should, however, note that Rhodes' reason for not wanting the complete defeat of Perseus was similar to Scipio Nasica's argument against the destruction of Carthage, and it reflects the general attitude of most contemporaries towards a powerful State. Experience had taught them that powerful States tended to embark on wars of conquest, and the best protection was a second powerful State; if Rome had not yet risen to the consciousness of a moral responsibility towards others, nor had anyone else; it was only when Rome stood pre-eminent that the Greek world became seriously concerned about the responsibilities involved in such a position, and then primarily because they were worried for themselves.

But if Rome was still groping towards a broader vision, she was not a mere freebooter. Though Rhodes was punished, it was not Rome who gained by it; the free port of Delos did not increase Rome's income.* The suggestion that Rome should make war on Rhodes illustrates again Rome's state of mind, a state wherein one cannot see that one's cause is not necessarily universally approved, and that other people may have different views. A more mature and cynical diplomacy knows the hollowness of so many pretensions, and may smile but keep temper if thwarted or opposed. But Rome was seeking nothing but security, and therefore did not appreciate the reasons for opposition to a policy which aimed at hurting no one.* Further, it may help to caution us from regarding the destruction of Corinth as a sign of degenerating morality; had Rhodes been as great a nuisance at this moment as Greece became by 146 B.C., she would probably have suffered a similar fate.

CHAPTER VI

PROVINCIAL POLICY

Rome regarded her provinces as extensions of herself rather than as independent communities whose welfare she held in trust. Her provinces had come to her from her defeated foe, Carthage, from whom they had been stripped, not primarily for their possibilities of wealth, but as a measure of self-defence. Sicily, Corsica and Sardinia were too close to Italy to remain in the hands of a hostile power, while in Rome's possession they provided an outer ring against attack. Spain was the base from which Hannibal had mounted his invasion; there could, therefore, be no question of handing back these possessions to Carthage. Rome therefore found herself possessed of these lands not because she wanted them but because she did not want others to have them; commercialism had not entered into her calculations, and she had no idea what she should do with them except govern them.

In Spain she was faced with the task of defence and settlement, and she set about this task in a thorough, unimaginative way, regarding it as an extension of herself and treating it in a similar way, without much regard for the fact that Spaniards were not Italians, had a different background, and had not reached the same stage of civilization. The time was still distant when Rome would regard provinces as a moral trust; for men of less civilization than themselves they had a contempt—or perhaps, more truly, a lack of interest and consideration—which, together with their absorption in themselves, made them indifferent to the minds and needs of the Spaniards or the Sardinians; and it seemed no more improper to them than to the Greek world to regard such people as chattels rather than men, and to enslave them if they would not be quiet. No ideal inspired them in the government of their provinces. Further, since there was no *ratio imperii*, many of the governors provoked rather than removed the causes of war between Rome and the hostile tribes outside her dominion; and while we may condemn the individuals, we should be more patient with the home government, who knew few details of Spanish affairs, and were not deeply interested in the uncivilized tribes who were the cause of the trouble. And, finally, the fact that there was no *ratio imperii* to guide the actions and policy of governors meant that the governors assumed their posts with little sense of responsibility towards those they went to govern. They were not imbued with a political philosophy which led them to a higher conception of their duty to those within their power, though the government maintained its high standard of honesty and incorruptibility, its own personal code, and strove—not unsuccessfully—to impose it on those of its members who fell from it. But many of those who went to Spain were unable to live up to this code when out of the atmosphere of Rome, and since they were infused with no missionary zeal towards their charges, they had no moral bulwark against the temptations of absolute power.

In this complete absence of a *ratio imperii* beyond that of defence and administration, and with the frequent wars against the untamed tribesmen, to which the Spaniards had to contribute their quota of men, with the uninspired nature of the administration, perverted by some governors who saw a chance of private profit, it is not surprising that the Spaniards felt little love for Rome, and resented the foreigner's yoke. The exploitation of her natural resources by foreigners, from which the provinces derived little profit, was a further source of resentment. They failed to win the allegiance of their subjects because of their attitude towards provinces and provincials. While they regarded the provinces as an extension of their territory, they were far from identifying themselves with the natives. Hence an alien administration, thinking almost wholly in its own terms, was unable to win the loyalty and respect of persons who did not want them or their way of life. There was little advantage to the Spaniard in being a member of Rome's Empire; and the circumstances under which the provinces had come into Roman hands and their Roman approach to un-Roman problems conspired to make the administration of these provinces a comparative failure, in the sense that they did not win the provincials' loyalty and failed to build a firm foundation for the future.

We see a similar situation in Sardinia. Sicily was a highly civilized and well organized community, whose administration Rome took over, making only such modifications as were necessary and convenient under the new circumstances. But Sardinia was wild and uncivilized, not lending itself to the quiet administration of its more highly civilized neighbour. Rome therefore dealt with it in her habitual way: Sardinia must be reduced to quiet and order, whether the natives liked it or not. And it was Rome's idea of quiet and order that was imposed; there was little attempt to adapt her outlook to that of the natives. The natural and logical consequence was the 'pacification' of Sardinia by Tib. Sempronius Gracchus, a process which consisted in the ruthless subjugation of the natives, together with the enslavement of many thousands of them.

This is an illuminating moment, for Gracchus was one of the most distinguished and enlightened men of his time; his achievements and conduct in Spain prove his statesmanship and responsibility, and his readiness, if possible, to appreciate the natives' point of view. No glib condemnation of his act as 'immoral' will help; it must be explained, it cannot be explained away. This was normal Roman treatment of tribes of little or no civilization with whom she came perforce into contact. She treated the Alpine tribes thus, the Epirotes, the Galatians, and certain of the Spanish tribes. The ancient world saw nothing wrong in the enslavement of primitive peoples, and the Romans employed these extreme measures when they were establishing settlements, as in the North, to ensure the safety of their frontier, or to safeguard their communications, as with the Illyrians; or, as in the case of the Epirotes, when they were determined to deny a potential enemy a strategic military position, because they thought their safety depended on it.

It was regular policy, not vindictive behaviour towards a particular tribe. And she treated Sardinia in the same way because Sardinia was Roman territory and she was determined to have orderly quiet there. The important distinction for us between Sardinia and the other tribes is that Sardinia was a province; and the fact that Rome made no distinction is a clear proof that to her there was no difference between the two. She was unaware of any peculiar responsibility towards her provinces, which as extensions of herself must be as peaceable as Latium, and if peopled by men of lower civilization must be treated as she normally treated such people. It seemed neither strange nor improper to Romans that the slave markets should overflow with wretches from her own province. So far had Rome's moral development to advance before any man within her dominions might say *civis Romanus sum* and in those words invoke all the majesty of Roman protection.

CHAPTER VII

ROME AND ITALY

The same limitation of responsibility is discernible in her domestic policy. Here the problem was different; the Hannibalic and later wars had brought about profound social and economic changes in Italy. The unsettling influence of long war-service, the effect of large quantities of booty and the influx of slaves, the destruction of farm property and the changing agricultural methods were all changing the economic basis of society. But here we must be careful. The ancient world did not recognize any but the simplest economic factors as such, nor did it think in any but the simplest economic terms. We tend today to think in terms of planned societies, integrated activities, balance of imports and exports, etc.; it is therefore proper in contemplating modern society to take account both of the economic facts and of the theories and ideas of society with respect to these facts; for they play an important part in moulding our society. The ancient world was only dimly aware of economic facts, was aware of their consequences without properly comprehending their causes, and tended to construct moral and philosophical theories to account for the facts and to suggest the remedies.

We must therefore judge them in their own terms. The growth of *latifundia* (large slave-run estates), the absentee landlord running his farm with slave labour, the conscription of the yeoman class for war service, were all combining to create social distress, and to take away from a large number of people their means of livelihood. The persons thus dispossessed came to Rome, where they contrived to eke out a livelihood as hired labourers in public works and as *clientes* of the nobles. This, we may say, was bad. But we must recognize that the newer methods of farming were more efficient, that the larger farm was a more economic unit than the smaller one, and that those parts of Italy which were given over to *latifundia* were thus put to their most profitable use. Secondly, we must remember that the dignity of work was not so keenly felt in the ancient slave-run world, and that, therefore, the social consequences of these economic changes were not felt to be so serious. Even in the Empire the *plebs urbana* was allowed to continue its aimless existence as the pampered drone of the Roman world. A rootless proletariat is a dangerous element in society, as Rome was to discover; some Senators were beginning to be aware of this fact towards the end of our period, when they tried to reduce the effect of massed *clientes* who voted in accordance with the interests of their *patroni*, by the introduction of the secret ballot. But the full danger was not seen, and even if to some far-seeing statesman the danger to the stability of society had been clear, it is difficult to know what he could have recommended. Since work was only a means to a livelihood, and those that came to Rome found such, there was no incentive to the government to find an alternative form of occupation. Nor is it clear what that form should have been; the ancient world was a very slowly expanding economy; the idea of producing more goods at cheaper prices to include a new class of purchaser is modern; such industry as there was in Italy was able to supply the needs of those who wanted its products. They had a balanced economy, but unfortunately it did not require the labour of all its citizens; it preferred slaves.*

The Romans therefore did not feel that things were out of joint, except from one point of view: namely, that the basis of recruitment for the army was property, and the reduction in the class of small farmers meant a reduction of those eligible for service in the legions. This was the aspect which struck contemporaries most forcibly, because to them it *was* the one important aspect.

From this point of view, however, the problem was serious. The army was the most important element in the implementation of Rome's policy of self-protection and consolidation, and the

Senate could not regard with indifference the reduction in the numbers of those eligible for military service. Two solutions were possible: either to change the basis of conscription, or to reduce the property qualification. The second was the policy adopted, but the progressive lowering of the qualification for the fifth class together with the gradual reduction in the value of money brought about in fact a change in the basis of conscription. The reform of Marius was only the conclusive step in a development which had begun a century earlier. The acceptance into the army of persons who had few and eventually no roots in the State would have demoralizing consequences, and enable the generals of the first century to use their armies as though they were their own. We need not here review the conduct of the army throughout this period; cases of indiscipline are recorded from the beginning down to the Spanish War; but the cause of the latter trouble was largely the necessity of prolonging service beyond the legal term. To this was added the demoralization which came of accumulated defeat and bad generalship in a war which to most of the soldiers had neither meaning nor necessity; and since many of the soldiers would have had farms of their own which were sorely in need of their presence, it is not surprising that the combination of defeat, bad generalship, lack of a cause, together with the relaxation of tension which ensued upon the destruction of Carthage, should have produced a serious lack of discipline. But it was very different from the indiscipline of Rome's later armies. The truth was that Rome's commitments were too great for her army system to sustain; the Senate continued to modify and adapt without drastically reorganizing, until eventually a wholly different system emerged; but it dealt with the problem according to its lights in the terms in which it presented itself.

Gracchus' attempted solution of the problem—also perhaps Laelius', i.e. Scipio's—was to settle people on the land in order to increase the numbers of potential recruits. In both cases it is probably true that they hoped to have a social as well as a military effect; but it was rather the solution of a philosopher than a statesman.* In the first place, all those causes which had operated to dispossess the original owners would operate to dispossess their successors; economic movements cannot thus be halted. If long service abroad had been one of the great causes, and if one of the reasons for settlement was to provide soldiers, then the plan defeated its object. And since the small yeoman could not under present conditions succeed, it was most unlikely that men who had not been farming for some time, if at all, should be able to succeed. We may compare the hardships caused in England by the Industrial Revolution; but the solution could not be a ban on the use of steam power, and a return to the hand loom.

We may see in the slow social and economic changes a gradual revolution, whose motion for long escaped the notice of contemporaries except where it affected the army, and to a less extent where it affected the voting in the assemblies; and in these spheres they tried to maintain the traditional status. When some of the social implications became apparent, they reacted as we should expect the ancient world to react, by following philosophical precept and going backwards. They failed and no one else succeeded; eventually the movement worked itself out, a new balance was struck and equipoise achieved. But the Senate's failure to provide a successful solution in the middle of the second century cannot fairly be adduced as an example of lack of responsibility or concern for the welfare of the State; it probably seemed to them that 'clientship' solved the problem for those individuals who would otherwise have been left to starve.*

Perhaps the greatest change in the social structure was due to the growth of the Equites to importance and influence as financiers and business men. Their rise had begun in the Hannibalic War, and had continued with Rome's development as an important centre of trade and her position as the most considerable city of Italy. The wars of this century required the services of contractors, the normal State contracts became more important, the Equites and the Italici began to roam far afield in quest of trade and profit; while such areas as Spain lent themselves to economic exploitation for those who were interested. The Roman governing class was not on the whole so interested, and, as we have stressed earlier, did not exploit political situations in the interests of Roman trade and commerce. This indifference enabled them to think clearly in their political problems with the outside world; but it prevented them from thinking clearly in their internal problems, where the Equites came into consideration. The Equites were rapidly becoming a highly developed business class, who took no part in Rome's government, and were untouched by those moral scruples which controlled its governors. The production of wealth was their aim, and within the limited moral code of their business they worked and flourished. Their rise in importance was another part of the slow revolution which was transforming Roman society.

We do not hear much of the Equites, and, when we do, it is generally because of a difference between them and the Senate. The Senate would gladly have stifled or restricted their activities, and did make occasional attempts to reduce their activities in certain directions; it could not succeed in holding back the revolution, though its slowness deceived them into thinking that possible. It was a normal development in the growing complexity of the State, as we can see; and the Senate would have been better advised to attempt by taking them into some sort of partnership in government to control them and imbue them with their own ideals. But commerce is not to a governing aristocracy of the land a part of government, and is generally frowned upon or actively despised;* and this limitation was to be found among the Roman aristocracy. It was aggravated by the political and mental outlook of the governing class, to which we have referred, an outlook which belonged to a city-state struggling to protect itself and to grow up, and to a time when the economy of the state was sufficiently static not to require the intervention of the government.

In consequence the Equites became a wealthy and a powerful class, with interests far beyond the confines of Italy, who, while they had no wish to govern, wished to exercise sufficient control over government to mould policy in their own interests. Through never becoming partners in responsibility they felt none; and since they felt none, the governing class regarded them with a mixture of fear and aversion, as men likely to upset the moral balance of the State. The political consequences of the Equites' activities eluded their uncommercial minds, both because they did not think in those terms but also because of their limited conception of their responsibilities as governors, and their unawareness of Rome's emerging predominance, which was imposing Rome's will on people for whom they refused to accept responsibility. Their attitude towards the Equites epitomizes the strength and weakness of the Senate: its concern for a high moral standard and its refusal to exploit the world, combined with an ignorance of the social and economic transformation that was taking place.

Rome's federation had on the whole survived the threats and blandishments of Hannibal, and had stood firm in the wars of the second century. Both sides were content with the relationship, which neither side had any wish to change. Yet slow, but subtle changes were taking place, some of whose manifestations were apparent, but whose underlying causes lay undetected. Rome, as a result of her wars and the influx of booty, with considerable building projects and the requirements of the army to provide work, was becoming a magnet to the citizens of many Italian towns, who began to be attracted in increasing numbers by the greater opportunities. The effect of this migration was felt in the Italian communities when they had to supply their quota of men for the allied army; they found it increasingly difficult to raise the necessary numbers. Both sides were worried and did what they believed to be the right thing: they ordered the return of the migrants to their homes. This was done twice in the earlier years of the century, at the request of the cities' governors.[1] It is interesting to note that here, too, it was the impact of the social and economic revolution on the army that made itself felt; and that the nature of the solution was similar to that proposed by Gracchus, to return the men in order to take them away again.

[1] In 187 and 177 B.C.

This was trifling with an economic problem which had social implications. But here, as in the case of their treatment of their own dispossessed citizens, both sides saw the problem only as military, and in their ignorance of the economic causation, they dealt with that aspect only of the problem that was apparent. In both cases it was the practical reaction of the contemporary world to the problem as they saw it; it is as unfair to criticize them for not handling the problem in the way we should as it would be to criticize the Athenians for not handling the plague in accordance with modern medical practice.

The high-handed behaviour of some Roman magistrates towards Italians should be regarded in the same light as the irresponsible behaviour of some magistrates in the provinces. Neither the former nor the latter was approved or condoned by the Senate; we hear of it because it was attacked at Rome; and its infrequency is perhaps demonstrated by the lack of official complaint from the Italians. It was the improper behaviour of a few persons, which is characteristic of States at this stage of development. It indicated not that morals were generally deteriorating, but that men of a certain character had scope to behave in this way, as they had not had in earlier days. In a period of expansion such incidents are to be expected, particularly where communications were such that a magistrate outside Rome necessarily enjoyed an independence which gave ample opportunity for misbehaviour. We may compare the excesses of some men in India or Australia at a time when none the less the British government, within the accepted limits of its responsibilities, was behaving in a way that none could censure.* It is useless to deny that some of these who went to India behaved disgracefully, and foolish to suggest that this was a symptom of a deteriorating morality. It was simply that the expansion of the State's territory required the services of more persons outside of Rome, and that more abundant opportunities for improper behaviour were provided for persons who would in any case have behaved improperly within more circumscribed limits.

The basis of the relationship was, however, changing. As Rome grew more important in comparison with the Italian cities, and gradually became the capital of an Empire, the Italians began to be irked by the different treatment and the disabilities under which they laboured in comparison with the Romans. In earlier days they had been content with their own citizenship and their relation to Rome. But with Rome's political and economic development, whatever the theory, Rome was in fact in a position of superiority *vis-à-vis* the allies. The allies continued to contribute to Rome's military needs without having any control of military policy; their citizenship, while still highly prized, did not carry the advantages of Roman citizenship in respect of rights and privileges; they were at a disadvantage in comparison with citizens of Rome. A spirit of dissatisfaction began therefore to be felt among the Italians, and a demand to arise for equalization of privilege, i.e. for Roman citizenship.*

The bestowal of Roman citizenship, however, to the whole of Italy was a concept new to Rome; she was still in mind and organization a city-state, and its wholesale gift implied a completely new conception of its quality, to which the adjustment must necessarily come by degrees. It would be the first step towards taking the whole Mediterranean world within her embrace, and could only come with an expanding realization of responsibilities. The admission of so many to the citizenship of one city-state would involve a completely different interpretation of State and citizenship, as granting a certain political status within a large political organization, as opposed to the traditional view that every citizen must be able to take an active part in the affairs of his city. Aristotle's limits of a State to the area within which a herald might be heard must give way to the dual citizenship of the Roman concept, citizenship of one's own city, local citizenship, combined with the political status of membership of Rome's Empire, Roman citizenship.

CHAPTER VIII

THE PROBLEM OF IMPERIAL RESPONSIBILITY

In this brief survey of Rome's attitude towards foreign States, to Italy and to her provinces we have been at pains to mark the limitations of her conception of responsibility, limitations which belonged to her stage of political development and resulting outlook. She was at the stage where she was the most important object of concern to herself, when she regarded other States and peoples as aids or hindrances to the attainment of her aim, which was security. This, combined with a considerable lack of self-assurance, explains the trend of her policy. But within those limitations, which were natural and not indicative of moral failing, the Romans showed a high sense of responsibility. The men who went to govern provinces and wage Rome's wars, whether against semi-barbarian tribes or against the wealthy and highly civilized Hellenistic kingdoms, had untold opportunities for irresponsible and improper behaviour. It was a time to test the homespun morality and solid worth of the Roman State. If Rome was interested merely in aggrandizement and self-enrichment, here were opportunities abounding; and if the State approved it, if its moral code was such that plunder and injustice were deemed permissible or praiseworthy, and if the moral atmosphere of Rome bred men to do these things, then we might rightly say that even within their circumscribed limits they behaved as irresponsible brigands, whose advance was a disaster to the Mediterranean world.

But what are the facts? Their conquests, such as they were, we have discussed; the chances for gaining new territories, the opportunities for seizing commercial advantages, were many; yet they showed a singular indifference to these prospects when they presented themselves. Certainly, at no time during these years was it Roman policy to exploit such parts of the Mediterranean world as came within their power. The peace treaties and their general indifference testify to this.

What shall we say of the individuals? That the majority of them behaved worthily of the *gravitas* of Rome. We hear of governors who plundered their provinces, of generals who exceeded the accepted limits of war in dealing with natives, of extortion, of electoral bribery, and these are often quoted as proofs of a moral deterioration. The first point, however, is this: that we know of these cases from Roman writers, because the guilty persons were either prosecuted or punished. Under the circumstances of independence which governors and generals in those days must necessarily enjoy, the cases are comparatively few, and when they were known action, even if not always successful, followed. The majority of the governing class maintained a high standard of moral responsibility, and tried to insist on the maintenance of its moral code. To say that some Romans fell from it and behaved unworthily is to say that Romans were human, and not all men are perfect. It was towards the end of this period that the first *quaestio perpetua* (permanent Criminal Court) was set up to deal with cases of extortion in the provinces; and this is itself a proof of the Senate's determination to maintain honourable standards of government. There are many examples in Livy's pages where the Senate took action against the improper conduct of generals and governors; and where it listened to complaints from the provincials and laid down procedure to prevent the recurrence of bad government. The greatest proof of the Senate's sense of duty and honesty within its limited framework is the testimony of Polybius; that part of Book VI which speaks with mingled awe and respect of the high standard of honesty and incorruptibility among Rome's governing class was written about 155 B.C., that is, towards the end of this period, although Livy can show examples of improper behaviour throughout the period. To Polybius the Romans stood apart from the rest of the contemporary world in their standards of honesty. That some fell from it indicates only, as has been said, that Romans were human; but Polybius' testimonial confirms that they were exceptions, and that the governing class strove on the whole to maintain its standards and punished recalcitrants.

There are passages in later books* which seem to remark on a falling away from this standard; but by then the general relaxation was beginning to make itself felt, while they adjusted themselves to the novel situation. It was not general then; Scipio and others were aware of the spiritual and moral problem; and to be aware is the first stage to solving it. Such solidity, so firmly founded, could not dissolve into nothingness; for reasons which we shall consider below the whole moral and spiritual foundation of Rome was undermined; but the governing class retained its high standards into the first century B.C.

The Senatorial government was aristocratic in composition, conceiving its first duty to be the defence and protection of its dominion, and this overriding consideration determined its whole foreign policy, its conduct towards the Italians and its provinces. Events and the progress of Roman arms brought about a gradual but profound social and economic change in Italy; the basis of agriculture changed, a new class grew up in wealth and importance, another in poverty and potential importance, and all this created domestic problems; in their method of dealing with these problems they kept rigidly within the framework of their city-state organization, dealing with what were in fact new situations, created by new circumstances, as temporary emergencies, for which they armed themselves with temporary emergency powers.* In this way they came to modify and adapt the instrument of government to its changing purpose, since what was done once tended to constitute a precedent for the future. They strove to maintain the moral tone of their society by preventing innovations in religion, thought or practice which conflicted with the *mos maiorum*. They clung to what they believed was best in Rome, and governed according to those ideals.

Within these limits—and we emphasize that they were natural and reasonable in terms of Rome's past, her constitution, and her stage of development—they showed a strong sense of responsibility in the execution of their duty; as a body they maintained their high integrity, and strove to curb the improprieties of their less worthy members; as individuals most of them behaved not unworthily of their forefathers. Considering that Rome was in origin and organization a city-state, had come suddenly to importance in the Mediterranean world, and had not the political experience of the Greek States, we should be surprised rather that their political instinct was able to adapt its organization to the needs of the time as well as it did; that was in itself no mean achievement and showed that, though conservative, they were not reactionary. They not unsuccessfully dealt with their problems, and once they had emerged from the moral and spiritual crisis created by the destruction of Carthage, they could have continued slowly and certainly to expand Rome's conception of her place and mission in the Mediterranean world. The thoughts of some were already towards the future, and others would follow; evolution is slow, revolution fast; but what is attained by the slow process of evolution is surely won, revolution seldom attains its goal. An aristocracy does not always fossilize; in fact it does so only when conditions become too easy. Rome's growing pains were sufficient to prevent any fat period of indolent ease. That sure instinct for adaptation by deepening the meaning of a concept without changing the words, which the Romans had shown before and were to show again, lay dormant in the hundred years that followed; and the reason for this was that their minds and energies were occupied by a more clamant question: Who was to govern Rome? And that irrelevant question was posed by the Gracchi.*

PART III

POLITICAL DISRUPTION

CHAPTER IX

THE GRACCHAN INTERVENTION

The history of the last century of the Republic is the history of a disintegrating State and society, in which men became selfish and self-seeking, while social and political problems became the tools of contending factions fighting for their personal power, and those spiritual and religious qualities which are both cause and effect of an integrated State were atrophied and died, leaving to replace them their material counterparts, greed and the lust for power and personal advantage.* These phenomena we shall later examine and discuss; but first we must study the history of the period since it was in the political sphere that the calamity had its origin, and the Gracchi were the men responsible.

Our brief glimpse of the period 200–133 B.C. showed the strength and limitations of the Senatorial government during a period in which Rome, through no conscious design, extended her sway and influence over the Mediterranean world, to become by 146 B.C. the most powerful State in that world. The transformation from a city-state to the strongest power in its world was itself the cause of difficulties; political machinery which was adequate for the administration of Rome in 250 B.C. was likely to break down under the increasing strains to which during these years it was submitted; that it did not was owing to the wisdom of those who controlled it. There had been also economic, social and political problems, the problems of Rome's relations with other States and with her own provinces and allies, all alike the result of Rome's unwilled growth to power; with all of these the Senate had grappled courageously, and with growing experience and maturity was feeling its way to a deeper understanding of Rome's new position.

The morrow of the destruction of Carthage marked the crisis;

the consummation of her self-defensive policy, the removal of the last supposed threat to her security, left a void in the political thought of Rome. She had no idea what she should do next, and since she had not yet awoken to the possibilities of assuming a responsibility for those who must depend on her, or of giving a leadership to States independent but weaker than her, for a time there was a relaxation of that tension which comes of having an end in view, with an attendant deterioration in the standards of their morals and self-discipline. At the same time the problems were still there, some of adjustment, others more basic, but owing to the seeming lack of urgency they were being temporarily neglected. In its approach to these problems, as in its formulation of a policy to suit the new conditions, the Senate needed to take stock of Rome's position and to readjust its whole outlook. This would in any case take time; it must be a gradual process, corresponding with the gradual realization of the new world which had come into being and Rome's new place in it. It would be impossible that every member of the governing class should feel the gravity of the situation, or that they should all brood at once on the critical future that lay ahead. A few would and did; with time the ideas of a few would become the property of a sufficiently large number to ensure that they were put into effect; and by waiting until that moment occurred, the State would be assured of the permanence of the new attitude and its attendant reforms.

Since 146 B.C., though little had been achieved, better men were thinking and their influence was being felt. The leaven of Panaetius' adapted Stoicism was working on the strong empirical genius of Rome, and from it might have arisen that cosmopolitan philosophy and sense of moral responsibility which came eventually after a century of bloodshed. Laelius had made a gentle effort to deal with the social and military problem which the economic changes had created; and although he withdrew his bill to prevent a schism in the Senate, that need not have spelt its final doom. Attempted ten years later, when men had grown accustomed to the idea, and with the support and co-operation of a majority of the Senators, it could have accomplished peaceably what it set out to do.* By trial and error, with good will and good intentions, the Senate could have dealt not unsuccessfully with the government of Rome. The twelve years between 146 B.C. and the tribunate of Tib. Gracchus had been years of sloth; there was an air of irresponsibility and aimlessness, a readiness by some to abuse Rome's strength for private gain, and an unwillingness to live by the high moral code of the recent past. This is familiar to us from Polybius and Lucilius; but it is wrong to see in it an irremediable deterioration of moral conduct; anyone who has read of the behaviour of many members of the English aristocracy in the 1830's,* and of the bigoted opposition to reform by such true patriots as the Duke of Wellington, will know that such things happen in certain circumstances, but that when the readjustment is made, the class as a class may emerge as sound of heart as ever. At Rome in 133 B.C. there were all the elements that could have made for a successful emergence from this temporary slough, nor is there anything to show that the Senatorial class were yet incurably narrow, selfish, irresponsible persons, as were the French aristocracy at the time of the Revolution. The spiritual crisis which the Gracchi caused has been overlooked, and judgement passed on the nobles because of what their grandsons were.

The city-state which had defeated Carthage was a compact society with a high sense of duty and an identity of outlook on the part of all its members, who were in their spiritual element at Rome and were proud of the State of which they were citizens. This continued to be true during the following years; and although in the ensuing expansion the State grew larger, and the feeling of being a member of one family necessarily made way for some broader conception, yet that broadening process took place without causing damage to the society. The concept of Rome was bound to expand with Rome's expansion; the idea of Rome as the most important city of Italy, which had replaced that of Rome as the most important city of Latium, must in its turn make way before the concept of Rome as an important State in the

Mediterranean world. With each broadening step the concept became deeper and less easy of superficial comprehension; yet the process had been sufficiently slow for mind and spirit to adjust themselves to the new situation.

We may take two actions of Rome, one at the beginning and one at the end of this period, to illustrate Rome's adaptation to the new situation during the second century. When Rome was brought face to face with Greece and the Hellenistic world, she was forced to define in some way her relation to that world, even though she involved herself solely for reasons of self-defence. Flamininus' proclamation of the freedom of the Greek cities was at once a statement of political policy and of Rome's new position;* it was an admission that in the quest for security she could not ignore the feelings of the other parties, and that she must stand for some ideal. We may admit that Rome's whole foreign policy was animated by considerations of security; that does not diminish the importance of the fact that she realized—perhaps unconsciously —that she could not achieve even that without an appeal to some ideal; Titus' proclamation expressed Rome's realization of her new, inescapable relationship and responsibility. Nor should it be regarded as hypocritical because in fact her self-defensive mentality was concerned only to keep Greece free of any power hostile to Rome. That was true; but it was also true that she realized that—to put it at its lowest level—she must offer Greece something sufficiently attractive to gain her loyalty.

In 149 B.C. was established the first permanent court at Rome, to deal with governors guilty of extortion in her provinces. This has for our purpose a twofold significance: it was a sign of some sense of responsibility by Rome towards her provinces, and also of her awareness that the relationship between herself and her provinces was permanent. Rome had not acquired her provinces through a deliberate policy of expansion, and, as I have shown above, she had no clear idea what she should do with them beyond govern them. Nevertheless, within the limits of her responsibility as she saw it, she was determined, as the institution of the *quaestio* shows, that the government should be fair and just to her subjects.* This was a good augury. The fact that it was a permanent court showed that Rome had accepted as permanent the provincial system, which, though it had begun as a necessity, was now to be continued and continued responsibly. The combination of these two ideals, implicit in the establishment of the first permanent *quaestio*, proves that Rome was still, as at the beginning, aware of certain limited responsibilities that went with her position. It was not clearly formulated in their minds; it was rather an instinct, developed perhaps in her past political experience in uniting Italy. But it was there.

This dimly felt instinct was important, not in its consequences, which were, as it turned out, slight, but in its significance. It played a secondary part at this time, and when there was a clash between self-protection and responsibility, policy was guided by the dictates of self-protection. It had not yet been brought to conscious expression, but such men as Scipio Africanus Maior, Tib. Sempronius Gracchus, Aemilius Paullus, Cato himself showed that Romans were aware that something different from mere physical strength was needed in establishing relations with other persons and peoples. Cato could express in homespun language something of what they felt; they could not yet enunciate a *ratio imperii*, based on some ideal, because they were not ripe for that; as yet they had none. Since the Romans were not thinkers, plans for ideal States did not spring in profusion into their practical minds; and that was good. For unless men are inwardly convinced, they are not won over to such paper schemes; and if a scheme's sole commendation is that it persuades their reasoning, a rival scheme may quickly supplant it. The Romans, like the English after them, tried to put on paper only what they had done, not what they intended to do; they moved instinctively along lines conformable to their society and the faith they held, and only afterwards tried to give the reasons for their actions. Frequently they could not explain themselves adequately; but that does not deny the faith that lay behind their actions.

This instinct towards responsibility was therefore of good omen. The morrow of Carthage's destruction was the critical moment; having achieved their aim of fifty years, they were left without a purpose. At what should their policy aim? They did not know, and, in the relaxed atmosphere of the following years, they did not think. Yet the seed was there and might have germinated; and with the fructifying influence of Panaetius' Stoicism working upon such minds as Scipio's there was no reason why this should not have been. They were slowly evolving a *ratio imperii* which expanded all that was best in Rome's tradition; no new way of life, but merely a broader one.

Such periods in a society's growth are critical; for while there will be a relaxation in morals and religion, it need not be permanent, and, given smooth and peaceable times, it seldom is. One may perhaps compare such moments in a society's progress to that of an express train when it comes upon the complicated node of lines at an important junction. At such a moment the train must slow down and, as it were, pick its way among the many lines and points; slowness and care will bring it safely through the dangerous complication to the open line where again high speed is safe. Rome had reached such a point, but a catastrophic chance brought the Gracchi to the driver's cabin; wherein lay the castastrophe it is now our task to discuss.

To understand the disaster of the Gracchi we must consider briefly the facts and theory of Rome's government at this time; for the tragedy lay in the means they adopted rather than in the ends they sought. Tiberius' aims were unoriginal; had his means but shared this quality, Rome's history might have been happier. The same may be said of Caius' aims in so far as they were those of his brother; but he went further, and the unintended results of his brother's means became with him a further end consciously pursued; to this extent he is the more guilty of the pair.

Rome was still governed by the machinery of the city-state from which she had evolved. Annual magistrates elected by the people exercised for a year supreme power; they were appointed equally for civil and administrative duties and to command Rome's armies, though war was rapidly becoming highly professional. There were only the rudiments of a civil service to provide the routine administrative experience necessary to control an empire;[1] while the junior magistrates attached to consuls and praetors were themselves learning their duties during their year of office. It was difficult for a magistrate to initiate a policy of reform during one year of office, and men tended therefore to carry out the normal work of their magistracy without attempting positive and possibly controversial reforms. But in spite of the inadequacy of such an organization to run an empire, Rome had not been unsuccessful; and this was due to the Senate, where alone experience and ideas could be blended into policy. By origin a consultative body, it had over the centuries acquired great powers, which had been conceded not only because of the social predominance of the *nobiles*, but because of the success of the Senate's leadership in the great wars. The Senate was the only permanent body at Rome, continuously sitting, not unwieldy, and well-informed; and in governing an Empire something less fluid than an annual magistracy is necessary if there is to be continuity of policy, if, in fact, there is to be a *ratio imperii*. Within the Senate was gathered the accumulated wisdom of the State, for most ex-magistrates became members; and by hearing its debates as they climbed the ladder of promotion, they acquired an appreciation and understanding of the problems which they would later have to handle.

It had become the custom for the magistrates to consult the Senate on all important matters; and while they could act against the Senate's advice, they very seldom did. For this there were two reasons: first, the practical wisdom and administrative experience contained within the Senate was such as to command respect, and the acceptance of its advice gave strength to the magistrate if difficulties followed. And secondly, the higher magistrates, who

[1] But what there was should not be underestimated. See A. H. M. Jones in *J.R.S.* XXXIX (1949), 38 ff.

came from the comparatively few families that constituted the governing class, felt a sense of loyalty to their class; to flout the Senate would have seemed tantamount to flouting their own class. Even more important, these dominant groups of nobles fashioned the policy which the members of their families, whose election to office they procured, were expected in their magistracy to carry out. There was a solidarity among themselves, not because they set their own interests above those of Rome, but because they identified the two; in their minds their good was Rome's good.

In this way a permanent and responsible form of government had evolved, which had shown itself capable of dealing with the domestic and political problems of the State. The aristocracy was at this time conservative but, except for a few, not reactionary; with their power and responsibility went privilege, and this fruit of government they would not lightly surrender. True, since 146 B.C. many of them had been enjoying the fruit without exercising the responsibility; but this, as we have pointed out, need only have been a passing phase. Until the Gracchi they had not been called upon to consider the surrender; they had assumed that they were the natural and proper heirs both to the responsibility and the fruit of government.

Yet their power rested on a very uncertain foundation. The Senate enjoyed its constitutional powers by precedent and usage;* if seriously challenged, it could show no writ other than the successful history of the last century to authorize or justify its present powers; it could lose all in an hour. It was just this challenge that Tib. Gracchus posed; he initiated legislation to which the Senate was in the circumstances bitterly opposed; yet his laws were passed.* He handled the legacy of Attalus, though it involved important considerations of foreign policy;* and the Senate could only look on in impotent rage. When challenged, they had not the direct power. Caius did the same; for two years he was Rome's uncrowned king, and, in whatever sphere he wanted, he revealed the Senate's impotence.

The Gracchi behaved, for whatever laudable motive, in a way that was fundamentally irresponsible. By using the tribunate as an independent means of initiating legislation they revived latent powers which had in the process of evolution long remained dormant, and which in the increased complexity of imperial administration should have continued dormant.* Only by adapting the facts if not the theory of government to suit the changing needs had responsible government been possible; by their behaviour the Gracchi undid the evolution of centuries. It was impossible to guarantee orderly government if one tribune after another, with all the personal differences of policy, could initiate legislation and deal with the highest affairs of State by bringing the business before a chance gathering of the Roman mob. There could be no necessary continuity of policy, and such a lack was fatal to imperial rule. Yet that was exactly what the Gracchi did, and with constitutional justification; and once done the precedent stood for all to imitate.

The effect on the governing class was disastrous. Conservative they were, and concerned, if directly challenged, to maintain a balance of society which gave them a dominating position. Any necessary reforms therefore must be gradual, and each step would be taken as its necessity became clear to a majority of the Senate. But each step would by that very fact be surely won and established, as having been granted by mutual agreement, or at least by a solid and accepted majority, not sullenly acquiesced in because it was impossible to interpose any constitutional opposition. Only indirect opposition was possible, and this could serve only to degrade 'constitutionality'. There were important men who supported Tib. Gracchus;[1] with time more would have been persuaded to their ideas or to the need for resolving the problems those ideas were designed to solve. Reformers who try to do too much too quickly succeed only in doing harm; had the Gracchi but had the patience to submit to failure, they would eventually have succeeded, as did the Reformers in England.

[1] E.g. A. Claudius Pulcher, P. Licinius Crassus Mucianus, P. Mucius Scaevola.

The Gracchi came forward impatiently with their schemes, as though alternatives did not exist, and by their methods they directly challenged the position of the governing class; and with that position went the accompanying privilege and power. Hitherto they had taken it all for granted; but once they saw the dangerous threat, the defence of what they held became their first concern. The problems of the State and the Empire began to recede into the background, to come to the front only to serve the interests of rival factions. The Gracchi put them on the defensive; their successors kept them in that posture. At once there grew up an antagonism, soon to become hostility, between the governing class and those ambitious persons who used the instrument the Gracchi had forged to serve their own purpose. They had shown the way to independence and irresponsibility, for tribunician legislation could not be a substitute for systematic government; while the Senate could only hope to succeed by developing a policy that would win 'popular' support, which in the circumstances of Rome could only mean to pander to the mob.

Caius had gone further; by organizing the Equites as a political power in opposition to the Senate, as he himself boasted,[1] he had further divided Rome. No one would dispute that the Equites should be taken into partnership in government; but to have set them up in opposition to the only permanent body, and to have given them power which enabled them to forward their own interests without carrying part of the responsibility of government, this was a piece of ignorance or petty politics, damnable either way. The Senate reacted as was to be expected; and while we cannot praise the Senate for its part in the events which led to the deaths of the Gracchi, we must remember that, as the Gracchi themselves had shown, the Senate was without direct constitutional power. All they could do was to invoke emergency powers, which had been developed for the co-ordination of Italy, for

[1] App. *Bell. Civ.* I, 22; Diod. XXXVII, 3, 9.

domestic purposes, and thus create in the *senatus consultum ultimum*[1] a further cause of strife between the Senate and its enemies. Their handling of the troubles served only to embitter the Gracchan followers, and sow seeds of resentment in the minds of men who had done no wrong.*

[1] A declaration of emergency by the Senate, which was generally supposed to authorize the magistrates to use any means against the public enemies; the right of appeal was temporarily suspended.

CHAPTER X

THE CHARACTER OF POST-GRACCHAN HISTORY

From this moment Rome's history took a different turn. In the years between 200 and 133 B.C. Rome had been an integrated State, a State in harmony. There had been groups and classes, each with their own interests and objectives; but these had never overridden the interests of the State. All men's loyalty was ultimately to the State, as embodying their own ideals and aspirations; if there was a conflict between the two, the State won. The Senate commanded loyalty as the governing body which implemented the State's aims; it returned that loyalty and respect by the responsible way in which it sought to carry out its duties. We have only to contrast the fate of Scipio Africanus Maior with the behaviour of Sulla or Caesar to mark the difference. Scipio, for all his claims to respect and gratitude, could be broken by the Senate. It did not occur to him to appeal to his veterans, nor, had he done so, would they have rallied to him. Whatever he or they might think of the attacks which led to his downfall, they were launched by members of the Senate; and since they won, he bowed to the storm and retired to Liternum. No such scruples or sentiments of loyalty checked Sulla or Caesar or their armies.

But now that harmony was broken; the State disintegrated into contending and hostile groups whose bitter wrangling and animosity absorbed their total energies. There were the Senatorial and Equestrian groups, each organized and having conscious interests, and the amorphous proletariat with its animal desires and its complete unawareness of having any responsibilities. Then came the great individuals, the Populares, who challenged the control of the Senate by their personal initiative, using the support of the Equites and the proletariat to attain personal ends. The

Senators fought for power and privilege, the Equites for power and profit, the great individuals for power. With every decade after the Gracchi men's minds grew narrower and more selfish, less interested in the problems of the State and Empire. As older men died, who had lived in the broader days of statesmanship, and younger men, brought up in the atmosphere of suspicion and hostility, took their place in the State, the atmosphere became more partisan, selfishness began to dominate, and responsibility became rare indeed; until by 60 B.C. the Senate was unfit to be Rome's governor, and the Republic to hold an Empire.

Herein lay the importance of the Gracchi. By the means they adopted they destroyed the harmony of the State, and by their impetuous haste put an end to that orderly evolution of government by which Rome had emerged from the chrysalis of the city-state to become the mistress of an Empire, and by which alone, even if change must now be more rapid, further readjustments could be made. Instead, irresponsibility, selfishness, mutual animosity and a profound disregard for all the problems of State and Empire gradually became the characteristic features; and in the growing discord the voice of responsibility was but seldom heard. The harmony of society was destroyed and disintegration began. The group, not the State, began to command a man's allegiance; victories were gained, not over the enemy, but over political opponents.

Disintegration involves every part of a society; a society cannot be politically disintegrated, while remaining happily harmonious in its other parts; either it is one or many. In a disintegrating society the State is replaced by the group, and such loyalty as there is is given to the group; and since the aim of the group is expressible in material terms, namely power, in the procurement of which almost anything is deemed permissible, the moral code of the society necessarily deteriorates, and what had been the expression of the society's aims and aspirations become mere catch-cries used alike by all parties for their own ends.* Men's spiritual horizon is lowered to the needs of the new situation; engrossed by the immediate environment they have neither time nor wish to look beyond the present to get a glimpse of some ideal transcending their petty quarrels, some ideal that can bring together what is sundered. The materialism and lack of idealism express themselves in selfish individualism; as group is more important than State, so, if there is a conflict, is self than group.* It is this lack of idealism, this moral deterioration, the selfishness and all the other consequences of disintegration which provide the key to the understanding of the Republic's last century, the moral and spiritual consequences of a political blunder.

As the struggle for political power became more engrossing, Rome's society of necessity split into groups with contending interests which excluded any common overriding interest. Men are chiefly concerned with what most nearly affects them; and this struggle so nearly affected all the contestants that it was impossible they should lay aside their strife to take counsel on Rome's Empire and her duty towards it. The whole Empire became involved in the struggle; the drama was played out throughout the Roman world; neither provinces nor external lands were unaffected by the convulsive struggle of the Roman classes. The provinces were sources of wealth; their government went, together with the Roman magistracies, to those who had at Rome the political power; their affiliation as *clientes* gave power to their *patroni*; they were the scenes of military triumphs and the sources of eulogy and distinction to those who governed them. In such circumstances the struggle for political power at Rome could not leave the provinces untouched.

External kings too were drawn into the vortex. Rome's supreme position and her expanding Empire left no choice to those whose frontiers marched with Rome's but sooner or later to become involved. Rome sometimes became the umpire in disputes; this provided opportunity to give decisions in accordance with the bribe; on the other hand an attack could lead, it was hoped, to military renown. Native tribes, however innocent and well-behaved, must fear to become the victims of some man's military ambitions; right was too often replaced by cynical opportunism. This was a gradual process, and while one may not condemn every man that governed a province, the unhappy truth is that, as time went on, an ever larger number deserved condemnation.

The magistrates, who after their year of office governed the provinces, were drawn predominantly from the nobles. To make money to recoup the expenses to which they had been put to acquire office, and to which they might be put by a political prosecution on their return, to indulge, if prospects seemed good, in some military adventure whose booty would enrich and whose successful conclusion would give fame and a triumph;* these were to the governor too often the objects of his government. Verres was but the most notorious of a class that went far to ruin the prosperity and incur the hatred of those they claimed to govern. Their suite consisted of young sprigs who hoped for adventure and profit; Catullus' complaint at his failure to fill his purse in Bithynia,[1] even though made in jest, is a commentary on the standards of the time. The wretched provincials were forced to bribe and bestow honours and laudatory decrees on those they would, if they could, have torn into a thousand pieces. The demoralization of the provincials, that was the necessary consequence, the loss of self-respect, bred a bitter hatred of Rome in their hearts.* Rome to them was the centre of political intrigue, the source from which came forth a procession of plundering Philistines, the strong undefiable power that held them in its awful grasp and slowly crushed them to death.

They had a further infliction; the Equites, one of the contending groups, hostile to the nobles, wielded vast power. The merchant princes and the large financiers of the State, they had both official and unofficial business in the provinces, as tax-collectors and as business men and money-lenders. Any moral restraint there might have been before was gone by now; profit was their only object, on as large scale as possible, to be extracted

[1] Catullus, 10.

by any means from provincials whom they despised.* Their political power was very great; their money gave them considerable indirect power, which they readily used; and their control of the jury courts gave them the power they needed over the provincial governors.* Most governors were happy enough to reach an accommodation with the Equites in their province; if they tried to consult the interests of the province, they were likely to find themselves in trouble, as Rutilius Rufus and Lucullus discovered. Between the governor and the Equites the provincials' lot was miserable indeed: it is difficult during these years to find any glimmer of higher purpose animating those whose responsibility they were. There were honourable exceptions; Lucullus and Pompeius both had higher ideals; Cicero was aware of responsibility; but when Sulla imposed a fine of five years' tribute on Asia for having tried in desperation to free itself from Rome's impious clutches, he behaved as most other Romans would have done.* They held their provinces, and although they were interested in nothing about them except their potentialities for plunder, for slaves and for honours, yet they were determined to continue their hold on them.

In such an atmosphere there could be no sense of loyalty to Rome throughout the provinces. As Rome became the focal point of Romans' interests, they had no time to spare for imperial problems; none of the problems that awaited solution received the scantiest attention; and younger men knew nothing but the Rome of political squabbles. Their minds became as narrow and as selfish as their squabbles;* at first there had been no time, later there seemed no need, to formulate a *ratio imperii*. The provinces were profoundly unhappy and powerless;* they accepted fatalistically what they could not escape,[1] but hated their captors for their servitude. Their worst oppressors returned to Rome to receive honours and lavish in bribery what they had bled from their province. True, the courts were filled with a constant stream of prosecutions; but these were not undertaken in the interests of

[1] As is evidenced by the Sibylline Oracles.

good government, nor in answer to a province's complaint, but to serve a political victory, to ruin a political foe. We need not be surprised that when salvation seemed at hand with Mithridates, the whole of Asia rose as one to put to death the hated Romans and Italians; and we may sympathize with Telesinus' bitter threat to raze Rome utterly to give peace to Italy.[1] The whole Roman world hated Rome; only fear kept them docile. Rome as the embodiment of ideals did not exist; it stood, a stinking cesspool of pleasure and corruption.

As they behaved towards their provinces, so they conducted themselves towards external peoples. Barbarian and less civilized people suffered as they always did, as a reservoir for slaves and an arena for booty and military glory. Rome's need for slaves produced the unscrupulous slave-dealer; men were kidnapped, whole nations depleted of their menfolk, with the same heartless indifference as were the animals collected to fight in the Roman arena. The same dishonest cheating and manœuvring to start a war or win a bribe impelled the Roman governors in their dealing with foreign powers; Mithridates' bitter denunciation of Roman perfidy was proved by his own experience;[2] Ptolemy Auletes could sway justice with his talents; Crassus could lead an army against a nation with whom Rome had no quarrel, and Caesar win a province for Rome merely to increase his power and *dignitas*. Such nations could not feel true friendship for Rome; they could only hate, despise and simulate.

There was no loyalty to Rome on the part of the provinces or the outside world. They knew that no sense of fellow-feeling or responsibility infused the minds of those who came to mulct them in the name of government; they had experienced the cheating and dishonesty, the crudeness and the insolence of those whose power they must respect. This does not breed loyalty but hate; and in breeding hate Rome was prolific.

[1] Velleius, II, 27, 2.

[2] See the account in Appian, *Mithrid.*, particularly Pelopidas' complaint, III, 15–16; also VIII, 54, 56.

Nor was there loyalty within Rome itself and Italy. In Rome men's loyalties were given to the group; there was no *patria* to claim their love, only a clique and a bribe. The nobles became narrower, more selfish and more unworthy of their ancestors with each decade; Cicero's letters reveal the feelings of one who had idealized the nobles when he was not one, and who had set as the pinnacle of his ambition to become one, only to find that in the truth they were far below his youthful estimate. He strove to infuse them with the ideals which he believed to be their birthright, in vain; and his disappointed contempt for their selfish insolence, their abdication from the duties of their station breaks out from time to time in bitter comment against those to whom their fish-ponds are their main interest. The struggle left them with nothing but a determination to cling to the power they still retained and to enjoy their wealth. It is the tragedy of internal strife that it deflects all effort towards itself; the governing class were blind to imperial problems, and they carried the morality of the forum into the world outside.

The Equites were no better. They had never taken a direct part in government, nor had they ever been imbued with the ideals of the older Roman nobles; when political power first came their way, it was at the moment when the nobles had relaxed their moral standards. They brought to their task their business ethics, which, adequate perhaps for their limited purposes under a government of high ideals, had not in them the germ from which could spring a moral code of government. Having had no share in government they were ignorant of imperial problems, nor concerned with them except where they affected their business interests; and their actions were directed to the promotion of those interests. Where their influence was felt, it was to forward their interests; what power they had was directed against those who at first opposed their materialism and lack of ideals, and later their growing power and influence, because it was aimed against them. It was Rome's ill fortune that business interests should become important at the moment of her moral crisis; earlier they might have been absorbed; later they might have been taken into partnership; as it was they brought an element of selfish greed into an atmosphere where it had opportunity to flourish.

To business men the profitable conduct of their business is their first concern; and this not seldom conflicts with the proper conduct of the State. To give business men political power without responsibility, when they are not imbued with the ideals of their society, and when their interests conflict with those ideals, is to court disaster. The Equites throughout this period exercised a pernicious and corrupting influence which quickly overwhelmed the nobles and made good government impossible. The massacre of Cirta was a testimonial to the hatred business interests had created long before the nobles had become indistinguishable in morals from them; it was chiefly they who dragged down the nobles to their own degraded code of money making.

The *plebs urbana* could hardly be expected to set forth some high ideal. It was composed of many elements: men and women whose parents or themselves had drifted into Rome during the agricultural revolution, labourers from Italian cities who had been attracted to Rome by the opportunities for work or idleness which the city provided,* foreigners and ex-slaves from all parts of the Mediterranean world, all the multitudinous types which a large city attracts into its maw; an amalgam of all nations and creeds, a rootless proletariat, to most of whom the traditions of Rome and her *mos maiorum* were never known, by the rest of whom they were now forgotten.

During this century they enjoyed a privileged position; for from them came the power which the politicians coveted. The *plebs* had always in theory enjoyed such power; but when the contests at elections were between nobles alone, when they said 'aye' only to bills which had been fashioned by the Senate, such power was illusory, or at least limited. But since the Gracchi had shown the way to independent legislation through the people, and since in the next decades Marius and his supporters had made them the instrument for legislation dealing with every aspect of imperial affairs, and since the Populares had begun to present themselves for office in defiance of the nobles, this power had become real. They were courted by all parties; bribes and legislation in their interest were the regular ways to their hearts and—what counted—votes. They became a mob, without self-respect or sense of responsibility; once they realized the power that was theirs, they used their advantage to the full. Held back by no restraints of upbringing, encouraged by those who used their numbers in their own interest, they became the hooligan mob with which Cicero has made us so familiar.*

In 100 B.C. murder and riot came easily to them; later they attached their services to one or another of the demagogues who organized their gangs to attain by force what reason and eloquence might have been unable to procure. They were a demoralized and dangerous mob of men, the product of their environment and time, which gave them neither work nor leadership nor good example; and if they were no worse than the nobles and the Equites in their selfish materialism, they were more dangerous. For having nothing, they feared no upheaval that might change their circumstances. The possession of property, as Sallust realized, was a deterrent to revolution;[1] the *plebs urbana*, not thus deterred, was the ready instrument of violence and revolution. It was the most dangerous element at Rome; and to its power nobles, Equites and great individuals had recourse.

[1] *Cat.* XXXVII.

CHAPTER XI

THE POLITICAL DISRUPTION—SULLA

At first the Senate might have seemed to survive the challenge of the Gracchi. It had contrived their destruction, forged for itself in the *senatus consultum ultimum* a weapon by which it might hope to destroy any imitators of their methods, and seemed to have as firm a hold on the reins as ever it had. This was but fair-seeming delusion. There was a bitter resentment among the Gracchan followers at what had happened; the Equites held the jury-courts, and being now conscious of themselves as an organized class could hope to intrude into the game of politics in their own interest; while the precedent of the Gracchi stood, constitutionally unshaken.

The Jugurthine War was to show the first consequences of the disaster. Our view on this war and the nobles' part in it has necessarily been strongly influenced by Sallust's monograph, and this is unfortunate. Sallust was writing in the last convulsions of the struggle between the nobles and the Populares, and his acute observations on the nature of the struggle and the character of the opponents gave him an insight into the truth behind the sham. His *Catilina* is in consequence an excellent descriptive analysis of the politics and society of the last years of the Republic, his own times. When, however, he tried to explain how this disintegration had come about, all he could do was to transfer the conditions of his own time into the past; because the nobles were selfish, corrupt and unfit to govern in 60 B.C., he assumes that they must have been similar in 112 B.C., and that everything that could be predicated of the rival groups and their quarrels in 60 B.C. was equally applicable to the earlier period. This is so far from the truth that his interpretation of the Jugurthine War and the domestic politics gives a false understanding of this critical period. The nobles were not corrupt and selfish, the Populares were not straining after efficiency against the treasonable inefficiency of the Senate; Senatorial government was still responsible, the Equites and their supporters were at this time the self-seeking and irresponsible ones. He did not conceive of a developing situation; as were the grandsons, so must have been the grandfathers. This view of Sallust's makes the *Jugurtha* as bad as the *Catilina* is good; he knew the grandsons, but had not the historical imagination to recreate the grandfathers.

A quarrel between two Numidian princes for the possession of the throne was only of limited concern to Rome, namely that whoever succeeded should be well-disposed to Rome and Rome's interests; it was a situation frequent on the frontiers of empires, as Rome and Britain have both realized.* Jugurtha's attack on Adherbal after the division of the kingdom, and the massacre of the Italians in Cirta created a difficult situation. In 113 B.C. Cn. Papirius Carbo had sustained a terrible defeat at the hands of the Cimbri, which had cost Rome almost the whole of his army. These migrating hordes on her northern frontier were a serious threat to Rome, and required the whole of her military attention. 112 B.C. was certainly no time to involve the State unnecessarily in a full-scale war in Numidia, where they were likely to become inextricably involved for several years, during which the Cimbri and Teutoni might strike dangerously at her northern frontier.

The Equites, however, were of a different mind. The outcome of a full-scale war would leave Rome in a far more advantageous position to pursue profitable trade and investment in those parts, and that was all that mattered to them. They therefore entered the arena of politics and so stirred up the people through the tribune Memmius that the Senate was obliged to name Numidia as a consular province for 111 B.C., and the lot fell to L. Calpurnius Bestia. With Scaurus on his staff he set off, and after a short shadow war arranged a treaty with Jugurtha on what were thought by the war party to be very easy terms. The truth was that Bestia and Scaurus had succeeded in making an honourable peace which saved Rome from becoming embroiled in an unnecessary war.

From now on things became rapidly worse; the Equites, foiled of their hopes, encouraged succeeding tribunes to attack the Senate, to criticize its policy and impugn the reputation of its members. Not content to bring Rome's enemy to Rome to give evidence against Romans, they encouraged the war by every means; after the disgraceful surrender of Aulus Albinus they instituted an inquiry which was so framed as to include not merely Aulus but all those who had tried in Rome's best interests to limit the war.* The Senate, which had been given no opportunity to take proper action against Aulus, was now put completely on the defensive, and was forced to pursue a war which served only the Equites' interests, at a time when the danger in the North should have been claiming all their energy. Marius and the Equites intrigued successfully to give Marius the consulship; by a tribunician law the command against Jugurtha was transferred from Metellus, who was doing a sound and thorough job, to Marius, who had intrigued behind his commander's back and tampered with the loyalty of his soldiers.

Meanwhile the bitter animosity which had been engendered between the Senate and the Equites made itself felt in domestic politics. The importance of the control of the jury-courts had become apparent during the Mamilian inquiry where the Equestrian *iudices* had condemned their political opponents of the war;* if the Senate was to govern, it could not have the powerful influence of the Equites ranged against them, and able through this instrument to command obedience; this was certainly government without responsibility. A bitter wrangle therefore developed between the two orders as to who should control this important political instrument.[1] A successful attack was made upon the nobles' hold of the priesthoods in order that others besides nobles

[1] The laws of Servilius Caepio and of Servilius Glaucia.

should be able to turn these offices to useful political purposes.* And, finally, the succession of disasters in the North led to a series of prosecutions of the unsuccessful generals, which culminated in a definition of *maiestas* such that unsuccessful generals could be prosecuted for harming the *maiestas populi Romani*.*

The Senate was being attacked on all sides; it had tried to study Rome's interests by confining the war, but unable to stand against its opponents, and thrown on the defensive, it began to look to its own interests, and to fight for political power. All the various groups with their own interests, particularly the Equites, were making a determined attack on the governing class; the governors were to be servants of the 'people', and give account of their stewardship to the 'people'. There was vindictiveness, self-interest and ambition in what they did; taught by the Gracchi that they could have power over the Senate and control policy in their own interest, they were determined to do so. Yet in such an atmosphere how could the Senate act responsibly? The Senators, finding themselves the target of attack, began to lose that assurance which governors must have, if they are to carry out their tasks, and set to defending their personal positions.

Further, whatever their intentions, the Populares had behaved irresponsibly in transferring to Marius the command against Jugurtha. If tribunes were to take it upon themselves to allocate important commands, then responsible government was in jeopardy. It would open the way to other ambitious men; and continuity of policy, the integration of strategy in war and a comprehensive grasp of Rome's commitments at any one moment would be surrendered to the ambitions of one man or the interested pressure of some group. On the other hand, it would be equally dangerous if men were to command Rome's armies simply by reason of their birth; yet all that the attacks on the generals were likely to accomplish was to make the aristocracy more jealous of their powers and privileges, and more anxious to guard them. The chief result of these events was to have shown the Populares what they could accomplish against the Senate in their own interest, and to make the Senate hostile to anything, good or bad, which had the support of the Populares, and particularly when a tribune was involved.

And thus we come to 100 B.C. In that year Marius, with the help of the Equites and his assistants, Saturninus and Glaucia, made a great effort to wrest the initiative in government from the Senate. This was the first attempt to use the consulship as a political instrument, and the example was followed by other Populares. The tribuneship was useful, and would continue to be an important instrument for obtaining for individuals what they wanted, and for agitation against the nobles. But it had not the tradition and reputation behind it which the consulship had; while therefore ambitious men continued to use tribunes to obtain what they wanted, they themselves tended to aim at the consulship, as itself conferring greater honour on the holder, and because for so long it had been held within a comparatively few families; the winning, therefore, of the consulship was a direct blow against the nobles and a mark of distinction for the holder.* Marius had the help of a tribune and praetor, who were to do most of the work, supported by the popularity of the successful general, consul for the sixth time, Marius. The Senate was not to be consulted, and if it objected, it would be intimidated. At first they were successful, and Rome was governed by the irresponsible Saturninus and Glaucia, appealing direct to the mob, with the moral support of Marius and the Equites. But the excesses of their hooliganism and irresponsibility frightened their most important supporters, the Equites, who had supported them only to forward their own interest, but were as unwilling as the Senate to see chaos and bloodshed in Rome. They, no less than the Senate, needed orderly government, and when they were disappointed in their allies, they instantly withdrew support. Rome was therefore saved from the worst consequences of this attempt by the Populares to govern Rome; but until their excesses had turned the Equites against them, they were supreme, and the Senate powerless. Nor was there any precaution the Senate could take against a recurrence;

they could only be fearful when a tribune embarked on independent legislation with a body of non-Senatorial support.

There was now a second object of fear; a general entering politics and supported by his veterans. One of the first objects of this alliance of 100 B.C. had been to procure land on which to settle Marius' veterans, the first veterans of the new type of army; and the presence of these veterans had undoubtedly helped Saturninus in the earlier part of the year, as other veterans were to help their generals' political schemes in the future. The Senate is often accused of having failed at this juncture to win the allegiance of the armies by taking to itself the allocation of land, in order that the soldiers should feel a sense of loyalty to the body to which they would look for pensions. Yet the problem was neither so simple nor so straightforward as this, and we may pause to consider the rightness of this criticism.

We may begin with this particular case. Marius in the eyes of the Senate had a bad record; his political intrigues with the Equites for the command against Jugurtha, which was the culmination of the attack on the Senate, necessarily left them with a feeling of hostility towards himself. The events of 100 B.C., in which consular and tribunician initiative had left the Senate helpless, thoroughly frightened them; and the hooligan disorders had shown the threat to orderly government and to the interests of the nobles which such behaviour entailed. It had made quite clear that its opponents were concerned solely for their own interests, and were prepared to flout the Senate and orderly government, if necessary, to compass their designs. There had been considerable use of force in preparing people to accept their legislation, and the elections for 99 B.C. had been particularly marked by violence and bloodshed. And since Marius' veterans had provided much of that force, they could not expect the sympathetic treatment which the Senate might otherwise have accorded them.

Marius had taken the last step in the creation of the new type of army* without reference to the Senate and without thought of the problems its creation would cause. Saturninus had then promised land on their retirement without consulting the Senate and without considering whether this was the best form of pension.* Even if the Senate could have brought itself to forget the animosities of the previous decade, it was not to be expected that they should bless this piece of legislation; it had been carried without any reference to themselves, as part of a concerted scheme for governing without, and against the wishes of, the Senate; and since the antagonism of the Populares was open, the Senators would reflect that Marius would acquire increased political power from the position of *patronus* which would be his in relation to the settled veterans. Had Marius not been in their eyes a rebel, and had he brought the question of a gratuity for his veterans before the Senate, something permanent and constructive might have been done. It was one of the tragic consequences of the Gracchan behaviour that questions of the greatest importance, when handled by the Populares, at once became matters of bitter party politics.

We may go further. As we have said earlier, a reform in the method of recruiting was necessary; it had been changing since 200 B.C., and the final step, which was taken by Marius, would have necessarily been taken in any case. Rome's overseas commitments and her colonial wars really required a permanent army, and there had been several cases of near-mutiny owing to the protracted service. Had the final step not been taken by Marius in the political circumstances in which it was taken, the general problem of the army might have been considered at the same time. The idea of a permanent army was involved in the general reorientation of which Rome's governors stood in need, but which they were never given a chance to attempt. The attitude towards the army therefore remained as before, that armies were specially raised for campaigns when a crisis developed, and when the campaign was completed the army was disbanded.

The idea of pensions was unknown at Rome;* it introduced a principle which obtained in no other sphere; and the question might reasonably be asked why it should apply to army veterans.* They had always had their share of booty; but this was different in kind and in addition to their share of booty. There may have been good reasons now for considering the question; but since the general and his army were in the Senate's mind at this moment inseparably involved in the political struggle of the previous years, there was not that calm atmosphere in which such complicated problems could best be worked out. Nor was it certain that a grant of land was the most satisfactory form of pension. Since many of the veterans would have had no experience of the land, it was possible that both socially and economically it was unsound; and the discontent of Sulla's veterans at the time of Catiline's conspiracy suggests that it was not universally satisfactory. And, further, where to find the land? It was not easy to find it in Italy without causing discontent among those who would have to surrender it. The discontent in Etruria at the time of Catiline's conspiracy emphasizes this difficulty. Nor would all men be ready to settle outside Italy, where land was available; the natural wish to settle in one's own country after campaigns in foreign lands could only be overcome by harsh dictatorship; though some would be happy to settle elsewhere, many certainly would not be.*

And finally, could the Senate, even if it had taken upon itself to provide pensions, have bound the soldiers to itself? Certainly not. This is the crux of the problem, and we may briefly state the fallacy of the contention, a fallacy which comes of regarding these years in retrospect. Historians contemplating these years from the standpoint of 50 B.C., and seeing Roman armies knowing a loyalty only to their general, ready at his behest to march on Rome; seeing further how generals entered politics to assure a grant of land for their veterans and used their veterans to forward their own political schemes, have worked back to the year 100 B.C., and have concluded that had the Senate taken the initiative at that moment, subsequent events would have been different. But this explanation fails to take account of the spiritual aspect. No man marches against his ideals; if a Roman army was prepared to march on Rome, it was because Rome stood for nothing that won their loyalty. As long as the Roman State was in harmony, and the

Senate was an integral and essential part of that harmony, the governing body in a State of which Romans were proud and which satisfied their aspirations, so long could the Senate command the loyalty of its armies and generals, whether it gave them pensions or not. But as a result of the Gracchi and the events that followed, Rome had begun to lose that harmony; and Rome, instead of moving as one to deal with its problems, became rather the political centre where a bitter intestine fight for power was being waged. Rome as the embodiment of the aspirations of its society receded before the Rome of political power and corruption. Men's minds became filled not with visions of Rome's destiny and responsibility but with ideas for outwitting their opponents; the State retreated before the group. Rome was the arena where the nobles, the Equites and ambitious individuals fought; and men gave their loyalty to one of the contestants. The armies were not loyal to Rome; neither were their generals; neither were the nobles, nor the *plebs urbana*, from which the army was partly drawn. The soldiers, feeling no loyalty to their country, gave it to their general. And if the only bond between the army and the Senate were to be the promise of a pension, then it would be a bond of thinnest gossamer; for the general had but to promise more, and if material advantage was all that kept them loyal, the general could outbid the Senate. The State had lost the loyalty of its citizens; it was given instead to the group. It is probably true that to most soldiers it mattered little whether they marched against the Gauls or Rome. They, like other Romans, were men without a country.

The essence of the problem of the army was spiritual, no different from the problem of disloyal generals, or from the hooligan irresponsibility of the *plebs*, or the self-seeking ambition of the nobles and the Populares; they were alike aspects of the spiritual failure of Roman society, brought about by the political disintegration begun by the Gracchi. In the political circumstances in which the problem of the army had arisen, the Senate could do no other than it did, nor should it be expected to have done so.

The next decade passed peaceably; the Senate, unhindered by

attacks on its prerogatives, gave Rome its last ten years of peace and responsible government until the *Pax Augusta*. It was, however, significant that in 92 B.C. P. Rutilius Rufus, the blameless *legatus* of Q. Scaevola in Asia, was successfully prosecuted for extortion in his province by the frustrated Equites, whose attempts to plunder his province he had prevented. It showed the difficulties with which the Senate had to contend in order to give Rome responsible government, and the evil influences which C. Gracchus had conjured up against the Senate. It showed that those business interests which had manifested themselves in the Jugurthine War were still working for their own purposes, even though the calamity of 100 B.C. had made it temporarily impossible for them openly to organize their own political machinery.

We must remember that disintegration is a cumulative process; by the year 90 B.C. no one under forty could remember the days of undisputed government by the Senate. They had been brought up in the atmosphere of mutual suspicion and hostility which was the legacy of the Gracchi, and to them politics meant that and little more. With each decade that passed the Senate became in consequence more narrow, selfish and parochial. This was shown in the crisis of 91 B.C., when Livius Drusus proposed the grant of Roman citizenship to the Italians. This should have been a problem of statesmanship;* but because it had been handled by C. Gracchus, and because Drusus was raising the question independently as a tribune, it was at once reduced to the status of a political wrangle, in which passion and insincerity replaced statesmanship. As the record of the Varian Commission shows, there were still Senators who thought as statesmen;[1] but in the urgent needs of the moment their voice was drowned. For the sudden addition of so many thousands to the voters would be likely to upset the Senatorial control over the voting, for which their *clientelae* were indispensable; and this was an immediate concern to them now that conflicting interests were seeking political power. They therefore

[1] E.g. M. Aemilius Scaurus, Calpurnius Bestia, C. Aurelius Cotta, M. Antonius, L. Memmius and others.

thought of their own immediate interests, and brought on Rome the Social War. And they descended at the end to contemptible trickery when they tried to cheat the new citizens of their rights by confining them to certain tribes, again to safeguard their control of the elections; politics had become partisan, and excluded statesmanship.

The year 88 B.C. witnessed the crisis of the Republic, and the crisis proved too great. Sulla's march on Rome put an end to all possibility of responsible government; from now on *fit via vi*. The Republican institutions were now a mere skeleton, round which each faction draped various trappings, claiming that they represented the true dress of the Republic. In this fatal year all the evils started by the Gracchi and the Populares combined to devilish purpose. Tribunician legislation interfered to dispose of a major command, the consul, Sulla, displeased with the change, marched his professional army* on Rome to obtain by force what had been taken from him by partisan legislation. Rioting and hooliganism preceded and accompanied Sulpicius' legislation, the consuls' attempts to thwart Sulpicius were forcibly prevented, thus showing once again that against a tribune and the mob the Senate was impotent.[1] The spiritual crisis had broken; some few there were who would fain have been statesmen; but most men of all groups thought now more than ever of their own advantage and interest. The bitter hatred soon to be manifested by the Populares, to be succeeded by Sulla's even greater bitterness and cruelty, is the final proof that Rome no longer stood as an embodiment of ideals. All parties were prepared to win their way by force; the armies were prepared to follow whosoever won their loyalty. The harmony of the State was gone. That Marius was the chief victim on this occasion is ironical, no more. He and his supporters had tampered with things whose meaning they could not understand; efficiency can be bought at too high a price; and even if we could concede that all they did was for the sake of efficiency, yet the

[1] And, be it noted, the consul, if he tried to work with the Senate instead of as a Popularis.

final result was the disintegration of the State. However commendable the original aims of Sulpicius may have been, when he used the tribunate to confer a command upon a *privatus*, he was making it the tool of a *dominatio*, and pushing to its extremity the Populares' policy.

Cinna used the consulship in a similar way. He sought not to conceal his autocracy; he named his colleague in the consulship, perpetuated his own, and gave his chief attention to scheming Sulla's downfall. This was open war, and Cinna developed Marius' use of the consulship as the means to his *dominatio*. It is not unlike the days of 51 B.C. onwards, when the Senate gave its whole attention to compassing the destruction of the Popularis, Caesar. Then, as now, the enemies at home plotted the destruction of the man who was doing most for Rome abroad; yet because party meant everything, Rome nothing, it seemed but reasonable that those who thought they held the power should prevent its seizure by their opponents.

Sulla's return and the civil war that followed ended the domination of the Populares, to replace it by the domination of the nobles. In the war and the ensuing proscriptions Sulla showed a brutal cruelty which served only to increase his opponents' hatred of the nobles. Yet while we may admit that statesmanship, if not humanity, called for mercy, we cannot wholly blame him if he visited on the heads of his opponents the penalties they had visited upon his supporters. Evil breeds evil, each act of hatred breeds a retaliatory act, and in this cumulative process there is a progressive degeneration. The standards of the year 81 B.C. were far below those of 132 B.C., and by 60 B.C. things will be twenty years worse.

Once safe in his position, Sulla showed no mean qualities of statesmanship. Aware of the need for stable government, he saw clearly why Rome's government had become unstable, and to the restoration of stability he addressed himself. The office he chose for this purpose was not without significance, *dictator rei publicae constituendae*. Cinna had abused the Republican office of consul by making it the instrument of absolute power; Sulla, with understanding and respect, chose an extra-Republican office to accomplish an extra-Republican task, namely to 'redraft the constitution'. He then reduced the tribunate to impotence, gave the Senate by law what it had enjoyed before the Gracchi by usage only; and did what he could to prevent a recurrence of his own behaviour in subjugating Rome by the force of his army. He gave the Senate what control was possible over the higher magistrates, and by laying down a strict *cursus honorum* tried to arrange for an orderly succession of magistracies, which would prevent their abuse by the Populares.[1] By making it treason for a governor to move or use his army outside his allotted province except with the permission of the Senate he hoped to keep the armies at a distance from Rome, and to deny ambitious men the chance to use them in their own interest.

The idea was good; the Senate, the only permanent organ of government in Rome and the repository of her political experience, was to govern the Empire; the irresponsibility of tribunician legislation,* fostered by ambitious men who wanted power, was cut off; the consulship would be an instrument of government, not of individual domination. Yet while on paper Sulla's constitution was commendable and seemed capable of providing responsible government, in fact it was foredoomed to failure. The animosities bred over the last forty years, brought to a festering head by the murders and proscriptions of the last decade, could not by a stroke of the pen be assuaged. The Senate was supreme because the Senatorial party had won; for that reason alone it must incur the hatred of the losers. In the unhappy circumstances one of the contending factions of forty years could not hope to command the loyalty of all; and without loyalty power was not enough. By now the nobles did not merit that loyalty; once secure in their power they showed that the buffeting of the years had taken away their sense of responsibility. Rome, with the Senate at the head, could no longer command the allegiance of Romans.

[1] Not least in preventing re-election to the consulship, the instrument of Marius and Cinna.

CHAPTER XII

THE POLITICAL DISRUPTION—POMPEIUS AND CAESAR

The events of 78 B.C. showed how precarious was the Senate's position. No sooner was Sulla dead than Rome was threatened by a Roman army under one of the consuls, Lepidus; and the only general to whom the Senate could turn to help the second consul in this minor emergency was Pompeius. Pompeius was a child of the civil wars; trained by his father in the art of war, he had of his own initiative collected an army which contributed not a little to Sulla's victory in Italy. Sulla had flattered and honoured him, and had looked on with easy tolerance at his youthful vanity and independence. He had ideas of greatness, but he was not of the stuff of which great revolutionaries are made. He nourished no schemes for remodelling the State; he was not a political thinker. He was a great organizer and administrator, and he could exercise his talents within the framework of the Republic as it was. His success and fame in the civil war made him anxious to be an important person, perhaps the first person, at Rome; more than that he never sought.

To him the Senate turned, though he was *privatus*, and entrusted to him an army with which to help to deal with Lepidus. This was inconsistent with the principles of the Sullan constitution, by which only senior magistrates, generally after their year of office, should command armies; and the Senate has therefore been censured by some for taking this step. Yet the precedent could have been good. It was only by flexibility and adaptation that the machinery of a city-state could be made to run an Empire, and thus it had over the centuries developed. One of the present difficulties consisted in this: that a man was elected to the office of praetor or consul not necessarily on his military qualifications, yet to him must fall the command of Rome's armies against her deadliest foes. The result had sometimes in the recent past proved almost disastrous to Rome; and there would continue to be enemies against whom none but able generals might hope to prevail. If there were at Rome some general known to be good, then it would be to Rome's advantage that he should be given the command, even though he held no magistracy. And if the Senate were to show a readiness to do this, it would at once increase the army's efficiency and its own authority. It could have been a step in the evolution of government at Rome, which while not breaking with the spirit of the past, ensured efficiency in the present.* Unfortunately, it was not allowed to become such a healthy precedent; in 67 B.C. the Senate turned its back on its own good example.

After his success against Lepidus, Pompeius was sent to Spain to help in the war against Sertorius; as far as Rome was concerned the years went uneventfully by until 71 B.C. Yet the years 78–71 B.C. showed that Sulla's constitution would not work, both because the nobles were unworthy and because their opponents were determined not to remain everlastingly excluded from power. An agitation for the restoration of the tribune's powers continued spasmodically during these years, which sooner or later must have some result. Joys once tasted can only be forbidden by force; the Equites were too powerful to acquiesce for ever in their powerlessness, and would eventually prevail on someone to restore their former power. The nobles, who could have negotiated from strength at this time, did nothing; what they had they were determined to keep, little realizing that if they tried to hold it too long they might lose it completely. Their conduct on the jury-courts illustrated how little fitted they now were to be Rome's governors; the trial of Verres, with its background of vicious intrigue and attempts to protect flagrant wrong and injustice, is a sorry pendant to the institution of the first *quaestio perpetua* in 149 B.C. The class hatred of fifty years had taken its toll; Rome held only selfish, petty politicians, determined to use their power for their own purposes.

The year 71 B.C. saw the beginning of the end of the Senate's honeymoon with power. Crassus and Pompeius, both with an army, both ambitious, and both jealous of the other's power, agreed to be joint consuls for 70 B.C. They therefore marched on Rome and with their armies not disbanded made public their intention. Pompeius was not qualified to hold the consulship; he had held no subordinate office and was below the minimum age, and therefore was ineligible. Yet his claim was not unreasonable; he had exercised *imperium* for over seven years, an *imperium* that normally went with either the praetorship or the consulship,* and he had received that *imperium* from the hands of the Senate. It would have been unfair and insulting to expect him now to start at the beginning of the *cursus honorum*; and if the precedent of 78 B.C. were a healthy one, then it was surely a corollary that a man so employed should acquire seniority in recognition of the time he had spent leading Rome's armies. It would therefore have been but fair that the Senate should permit his candidature. The Senate, however, acted through a sense not of justice but of fear; the armies on the outskirts of Rome had an eloquence denied to Pompeius' claims. And here we see the failure of Sulla's precautions; one cannot replace loyalty by law. If men were ready to march on Rome, no law could hold them back. The Senate was hated as much as ever, and Rome had no attractive force upon the spirits of its citizens.

Pompeius and Crassus had pledged themselves to remove from the tribunate the last of the Sullan disabilities; and they contrived to agree long enough to redeem their pledge. Thus was the situation restored to pre-Sullan times; there was this difference, that for ten years the Senate had exercised sovereign power without making any effort to heal the breaches between the classes; it had shown little sense of responsibility, and had used the years and the power chiefly in its own interests. The nobles lost their monopoly of the jury-courts, for which they had shown themselves no better fitted than the Equites. This was the end of Sulla's attempt to create a workable Republican constitution, an attempt doomed from the outset by the past, which could neither be undone nor forgotten.

Pompeius had restored to the Populares their independence; the nobles, who when untrammelled by the tribunate had shown no statesmanship, and would now be more than ever selfish and concerned to defend their privileged position, were soon put to the test. In 67 B.C. the tribune Gabinius passed a law which gave Pompeius very considerable powers against the pirates. The Senate, led by two of its greatest members, Catulus and Hortensius, unsuccessfully opposed the bill. This was the crisis of their affairs in the post-Sullan world, the crisis which showed their incapacity to rule.

The pirates had for many years been a menace to commerce and shipping; twice the Senate had appointed commanders to deal with them, and twice the Republic had had to confess itself defeated. Cicero has described the state of the seas and the coastal parts of the Empire at this time;[1] even the corn supply was in jeopardy. Immediate and energetic action was needed, and it was the responsibility of those that called themselves governors to take that action. The Senate had its own precedent of 78 B.C. for appointing a *privatus* to command in time of danger. Pompeius' military record was such as to give him claims to such a command; yet in spite of their own precedent, the present danger and Pompeius' record they fought against the appointment. We can see why they did, because they feared Pompeius as a Popularis; and since the animosity between the groups was even more bitter than before, the one side because it had lost its exclusive powers, the other because it was at last able to take revenge for ten years' impotence, it was sufficient that a tribune was passing a law in favour of Pompeius for the Senate to oppose it. Yet their own failure to grapple with a serious problem, their refusal to use the talent within the State, and their opposition to a bill which aimed to make good their deficiencies, meant simply that the restored tribunate could be capable of greater responsibility than the Senate.

[1] *De Pomp. Imp.* 32–5.

This is the one side of the Senate's failure at this moment; the other side is shown in Sallust. On the one side we have the failure to rise to the responsibility which should have been theirs; this was the negative aspect. But there was worse than that; since Pompeius in their despite had left Rome, as it turned out for some years, the nobles, having failed to prevent the resurgence of the Populares, used the opportunity of Pompeius' absence to strengthen their position by repressing and intimidating the Populares while they were without a leader.* No thought of statesmanship, merely of safeguarding their position against the new threat. And so it was that when Pompeius returned at the end of 62 B.C. he found a close-knit opposition to contend with.* Here was the final proof that the nobles were unfitted to command; to this the Gracchan experiment with time had brought a once proud and honourable organ of government. Only a power stronger than any of the contending parties could by imposing a discipline upon them, restore a unity to the State which would make responsible government possible.

The last years until the outbreak of the civil war need not detain us long. The Senate organized itself against Pompeius' return, and Cato was their mouthpiece. Pompeius' achievements against the pirates and in Asia were by any standard great, and had contributed to the safety, welfare and wealth of the State. On his return he demobilized his army and came to Rome, with two requests to make of the Senate, refusal of which would be a personal insult and a degradation to a Roman Imperator. He asked for the ratification of his Eastern *acta*, and land for his veterans. It was the plain duty of the government to expedite both these requests.* The Senate, if it claimed to govern, must do so; it was palpably unfair and improper to leave large territories in doubt as to their future organization and administration. The question should have been dealt with at once, any necessary changes made, and the arrangements then ratified. Similarly, since the granting of land had now become the accepted form of military pension, and since, during their years of supremacy they had not attempted to handle the problem of the army or of its pensions, they had an obligation to grant to Pompeius' successful and well-behaved soldiers what they had been accustomed to give to other veterans. But because most nobles hated and feared Pompeius, because without his army he was powerless, because ten years earlier he had frightened them and seemed to play the demagogue, and because he had been before his departure the rallying point of their opponents, they preferred, now that he seemed within their power, to play petty politics with important matters of State, and humiliate Pompeius by deliberately procrastinating. They succeeded in humiliating Pompeius, dishonouring themselves and bringing ruin upon their own heads.

Their opposition to the request of the *publicani* for a remission of their contract price, and their attempts to thwart Caesar, brought Crassus and Caesar together with Pompeius into the first triumvirate.* The Senate's attempt to oppose Caesar's legislation proved vain; the consul with tribunician aid, supported by the Equites and Pompeius' veterans, could do exactly as he wished; the weapons forged by the Gracchi and Marius showed their strength; the Senate had only epigrams with which to parry the strokes.[1] Even though the mob began to turn against them, yet they were all-powerful, the real *dominatio* of the Populares.

Nor could the Senate recover its position by challenging the legality of Caesar's legislation; this had been the Senate's main redress in the past, but it failed now. It had succeeded before because the coalition which had been responsible for the legislation had broken up in the crisis that followed; on this occasion the coalition held; the conference at Lucca re-established the triumvirate, and Pompeius and Crassus returned to Rome to execute their plans. The details of those plans need not concern us here; the Senate perforce looked on while the triumvirate divided the Roman world to its satisfaction. During the whole of this time the triumvirs' only concern had been for power; by what means

[1] Bibulus had to content himself with publishing epigrammatic edicts; see Cic. *Ad. Att.* II, 20, 6; 21, 4.

they won and held it they cared not. In the progressive disintegration of the State, as the struggle for power became more open and all-important, hooliganism and the force of the mob and organized gangs came to play an increasingly decisive role in the politics of Rome; and these aids to power the triumvirate had used with good effect. In the absence of any strong hand at Rome hooliganism had now grown out of control; the year 53 B.C. opened without consuls, and again the year 52 B.C. Things had grown so bad that either strong action must at once be taken, or a complete breakdown of government must be expected. A strong man must be named to restore order and ensure orderly elections. And, as in 78 B.C., the Senate had no one among its loyal members with the ability for this purpose; Pompeius there was at Rome, if he could be trusted. Senate and Pompeius were forced together again, after two decades of separation which need not have been. Pompeius was given the chance to be the first man in the Roman Republic; more than that he had never sought, and the Senate could have had his alliance and the strength of his prestige from the moment of his return from Asia, had they had the wit and statesmanship to do their duty. Pompeius was not a revolutionary by nature but of necessity; he had been uneasy in his unholy partnership of 59 B.C., but he had been forced into it, and once committed he could not withdraw. Further, he had felt that Caesar, not he, was the leader, and had shuffled uneasily at his inferiority; now the opportunity had come to escape from his unhappy alliance and be the first man in the Republic. After deliberation Pompeius was named sole consul, the suggestion of a dictatorship having been dismissed by Bibulus, who claimed that a sole consulship was less un-Republican.

It is interesting to reflect on the reasons which perhaps induced Bibulus and Cato to this conclusion. At first sight a sole consulship might seem to be a negation of the Republic, wherein duality and an equal sharing of the *imperium* were cardinal. The old style of dictatorship was dead since the second Punic War, and could not be revived now, since Sulla's dictatorship had intervened, and dictatorship must necessarily now carry with it the additional implications which it had acquired from Sulla's tenure of the office. What, then, were these implications? Most important, its timelessness. Sulla had remained dictator as long as he chose, and as such stood above the whole Republican constitution; thus he could have remained until his death. The Senate was still far from feeling that complete confidence in Pompeius which would let them clothe him with an office which only he could doff. Caesar's remark on Sulla's abdication of the office[1] and his own use of it show that men were aware of the possibilities of the Sullan dictatorship. Secondly, Sulla had used the office to redraft the constitution;* true, it had been in the interests of the Senate, but if Pompeius were to try his hand at changing the constitution to put an end to the present chaos, they could not feel certain that the man who had restored the tribune's rights would now respect the nobles'. They did not seek any change in the constitution, even for the better; in its present form they still had considerable power and indirect control; all they wanted at this moment was an end of anarchy, in order that they might continue to exercise what power they had. If Pompeius would be their friend so far, they wanted no more.

What, then, of their own instrument, with which they had been wont to quell civil disorder in the past, the *senatus consultum ultimum*? They had passed the *senatus consultum ultimum* and entrusted the *interrex*, the tribunes and Pompeius with the task of restoring order, but the crisis called for more than the quelling of disturbance; they had eventually had consuls in 53 B.C. but that had not prevented violent disturbance. They needed at this moment a strong man. Full authority must be given to someone, yet that authority must be limited in time and competence. The consulship since the days of Marius could be a dangerous office, as Cinna and Caesar had shown; yet it was annual, and since the time of Sulla there had been no case of the multiplied consulships of Marius and Cinna. There was a risk, but far less than that

[1] Suet. *Iulius*, 77.

involved in a Sullan dictatorship, and they still exercised a considerable control over elections, if they could be held. And, secondly, a consul was a constitutional officer; if he wished to change the constitution, he would have to proceed by normal means of legislation, which while they might be as irresponsible as the means used by the Populares in the past, might perhaps be balked, or perhaps repealed after Pompeius' year of office. But, more important, under the circumstances of his appointment as the nominee of the Senate it would be difficult to turn against them; he had not since 70 B.C. been a leader of anti-Senatorial legislation; he had made but a half-hearted attempt in 60 B.C. to use a tribune, and had taken only an embarrassed and passive part in the events of 59 B.C.; in the negotiations which must have preceded this appointment he had probably expressed a readiness to serve the Senate—or at least not to turn against them. Pompeius was therefore endowed with the sole consulship in the hope that he would save the nobles. The fact that some such office was recognized to be necessary was an indication of the need either of some emergency office such as the old dictatorship, or of some permanent officer endowed with the prestige and the power to guarantee the harmonious working of the constitution, since it was by now clear that it could not be guaranteed to work otherwise; both groups were prepared to go to any length in their own interests.

The alliance with Pompeius continued, and Pompeius led the nobles in their final fight for power against Caesar, the greatest of the Populares. The Republic had long been dead; the fight was unashamedly for power, as it had been for many decades, between two rival groups, one of which used the name of the Republic as its watchword;* but the Republic for them represented only that system of government which gave them the power and the privilege. It was no ideal of Rome to which they summoned their supporters, for ideals had long passed from men's minds. Only at the end of this unhappy period was a rallying cry to be found in the threat of an outside power, East versus West; and thus the unity which Octavianus won was the restored unity of the days before Carthage's destruction,* and Augustus was to take up the task from there, to carry on what the Gracchi had delayed a century.

We may in closing this brief survey consider the two leading characters of this last act, Caesar and Cato. Caesar was a man of great ambition, to which was added all the genius of natural parts. His political life until 60 B.C. had been neither better nor worse than that of most of his contemporaries. He had employed the arts of bribery, amassed huge debts in consequence, and been ready to join in political schemes by which he might hope to increase his personal power. He had contrived never to become so hopelessly embroiled that he was compromised by their failure; and by a judicious mixture of charm and bribery he had won his way to the chief priesthood and the praetorship. He then sought the consulship, the consulship as it had been fashioned by the Populares; his political past ensured the opposition of the nobles. When their opposition failed in that and their attempt to deny him a proper province was foiled, they tried to prevent the passing of his legislation, though nothing they could do could thwart its passage; the Populares knew how to control the constitution. When he was gone to Gaul they tried unsuccessfully to thwart and ruin him; and from 51 B.C. onwards, when they had Pompeius on their side, the end of all their schemes and machinations was the political death of Caesar. This became the supreme object of Rome's governing class, to the exclusion of all the many problems of State and Empire that should have weighed upon them: to destroy Caesar. He was a Popularis, he had flouted them, he was great, and therefore he must go.

Caesar was a genius, and a well-ordered State should be able to employ its great men fruitfully. If Caesar climbed to power by opposition to the nobles, it was because he could never have succeeded without it. Their opposition to Pompeius and to Caesar proved their incapacity to rule; Rome's greatest men must oppose the government in order to help Rome, and then must pay the penalty for that opposition. Caesar was the child of his times; had he not been, he never would have succeeded. He could see how contemptible were the nobles, and he treated them accordingly. But that he should have been forced to become a revolutionary, leading his army against his country, was the nobles' fault, not his; the crossing of the Rubicon was their not his condemnation. His words on the field of Pharsalus express the truth,[1] and the truth was an indictment of the cliques who had run the Empire as a private estate.*

The leader of the nobles was Cato. History has been kind to Cato; his suicide sanctified him in the eyes of the Imperial Stoics, and his association with the Republican cause as a sorry idealism pictured that cause to the victims of the tyranny of Emperors, endowed him with an air of holiness which neither he nor it ever wore at the time. Cato was good, but he was far from great. He was honest and principled beyond the normal standards of the day; but he had not that vision and understanding, that flexibility of mind, and those qualities of statesmanship by which alone the Republic could be saved.* It was Cato who opposed Pompeius' requests in 60 B.C., it was Cato who led the opposition to the request of the *publicani*, it was Cato who forced Caesar to ignore the Senate with his legislation. He more than any other created the triumvirate, that combination of three Populares who might separately have been appeased or checked. In truth his vision was no wider than that of his fellow-nobles; his ideal was government by the Senate, in pursuit of which ideal he led the opposition to all who challenged it. He could not see that the challenges were symptoms of a deeper distemper; the spiritual problem passed unnoticed; himself punctilious in form and honesty, he was content to fight for a system which respected neither the form nor the spirit of the Republic, whose proponents were selfish and dishonest; he was content that a system of patronage which could and did exclude much of the ablest talent should be perpetuated in the sacred name of the Republic. He was, in fact, an honest member of the noble Senatorial class, and nothing more; for the gigantic

[1] Plut. *Caesar*, XLVI, 1; Suet. *Iulius*, 30.

task of leading the nobles and so guiding their policies that they should adapt themselves to present needs he was wholly unequipped. He was their figurehead rather than their leader. He could give by his death a glow of idealism to the rotten corpse of the Republic, which hid from men's eyes the corruption that was beneath. In truth the Senate could not have brought about its own salvation; had Cato been a greater, nay, a great man, he would have been in Caesar's ranks.

PART IV

THE CONSEQUENCES OF DISINTEGRATION

CHAPTER XIII

THE SOCIAL CONSEQUENCES

The consequences of the growing political disintegration could not hope to be confined to the Forum; and indeed they were to be seen in the moral and religious degeneration of society during this century. Instead of the self-discipline of earlier times, we find an almost total lack of restraint on the part of most men and women in the attainment of their wishes and a reluctance or refusal to submit to the discipline of society; selfishness and individuality are the dominant traits of this period, combined with a growing lack of moral self-control, the result of the loosening grip of Roman religion and the Roman code of morals. These phenomena we may now examine more closely.

When men for a purpose surrender their ideals, those ideals are lost to them; when men for a purpose sink to selfish and immoral conduct, that conduct becomes their way of life. The bad behaviour in politics could not hope to find compensation in high-principled behaviour where politics were not involved. The exigencies of politics destroyed the best in these men's characters. We find therefore all the weakness and the rottenness of the political arena permeating every corner of Rome's social life; and to this we may now briefly turn.

A description is by its nature static, whereas society is not. Roman society was worse in 60 B.C. than it had been in 90 B.C.; a general description of this society will necessarily refer to certain aspects which belong only to the later date. None the less, a general description is in this case possible; the difference was only of degree, not of kind. The disintegration was a process which continued along its predestined lines from its first small beginning to its unhappy conclusion; the year 60 B.C. was therefore but a more advanced form of 90 B.C.; and for our purposes it is sufficient to describe in general terms the disintegrating society without over-due concern as to when a phenomenon first manifested itself.

Selfishness, absence of moral sanctions, positive dishonesty were the characteristics of the groups at Rome; and these same characteristics were to be found in private life. Further, lack of spiritual faith and a moral code led to gross materialism, a tasteless extravagance and ostentation far removed from the cultured balance of a healthy society. This was shown in men's attitude to money and debts. Political life became more expensive as the scale of bribery became greater. The bribery laws were dead, and bribery for electoral purposes was open and unashamed. Nor did bribery take only the direct form; a young aspirant to office must bring himself before the people and court popularity, and this he did by spending lavish sums on public entertainment in his aedileship. Young men contrived without a qualm to accumulate a staggering load of debt at the outset of their careers, which could be recouped only by loans or by a lucrative governorship; many political careers looked ultimately to a province not merely to restore a man's shattered finances, but to provide a fortune for his remaining years.

This attitude to money, wherein one felt no constraint to live within one's means, bred a similar attitude to property in general. A selfish desire to be possessed of material things, whether one could afford them or not, led to debt and, in the fast deteriorating atmosphere, to covetousness. When the chance presented itself, too many were ready to bring about the ruin of friend or foe to possess themselves of his estate or villa. Luxurious villas and town houses ate up fortunes; millions of sesterces were spent on the pleasures of the table and on highly qualified slaves.

This immoral attitude towards money and this weak surrender to the satisfaction of material desires was itself bad and bred further ills. The law of debt could still be harsh at Rome; many persons found themselves loaded with debt and beholden to a creditor who knew no mercy. Among a large class there was therefore a spirit of hopelessness and despair, which found refuge in revolution. Laws to alleviate debt, cries of *novae tabulae*, are discerned at intervals throughout the period; among Catiline's supporters were debtors who hoped for revolution to free themselves of debt and perhaps acquire a fortune in the bloody confusion that would ensue. Many of these debtors were the younger members of noble families;[1] brought up in the moral squalor of Rome, not educated to revere Rome's old traditions, and seeing those around them devoid of scruple and respect, forced by their birth to the extravagancies of public life, they found themselves too often ruined before they began. Not all young men had Caesar's genius to emerge from debt.

It was not merely that in this general demoralization the coarse pleasures of the voluptuary became sought after; the essential vulgarity of the Roman had full scope. As in Hollywood, 'terrific', 'colossal' seemed terms of praise, and without the inherent taste which sets a mean in such matters, whether it was a villa or public games that were in question, the chief criterion was size. The wanton destruction of human and animal life in the arena bred a callousness and contempt for individual life, which was encouraged by the despotic rights of masters over their slaves, and the cruel and humiliating circumstances under which so many slaves were held. A coarse vulgarity was seen in the popularity of the newer forms of drama, which had ousted the early drama, based on Greek models. The shameless crudity which was to disgrace the stage under the Empire began now, when at all costs the Roman mob must be amused, whether the entertainment was worthy of Rome or not. And when Roscius carried among his baggage on the expedition against the Parthians a book of Milesiaca,[2] we may know that the wealthier classes were capable of the same low tastes.

Loose sexual relations became common. We cannot infer too much from the divorces of which we read; Romans sought

[1] Cf. Sallust, *Cat.* XIII, 4; XVII, 6: ceterum iuventus pleraque *sed maxime nobilium* Catilinae inceptis favebat. See also XLIII, 2.

[2] Plut. *Crassus*, XXXII, 3.

divorce for many reasons besides infidelity, and even for no reason. But the frequency of divorce for trivial or dynastic reasons reflected an easy tolerance towards the married state, which must be harmful if not fatal to the sacredness of family life, on which Rome's earlier greatness had so much depended. Women became important in the background of political life; this, in so far as it represented a social development which gave women an honourable place outside as well as inside the family, was to be commended. But it was only to a limited extent such a development; women were still betrothed in their early teens, divorced and handed over to others for dynastic reasons; in such circumstances there can be no honourable place in the larger sphere of society for women. Sometimes they might be truly loved by their husbands, as Julia was; then they might hope to exercise an influence, if their husbands were figures of importance. More often a woman won her position by her force of character, as did Servilia;[1] it was a tribute to her personality rather than to her sex.

But the influence that women undoubtedly wielded behind the scenes was due to the looser relations which sprang up between the sexes at this time, such as is depicted for us by Ovid in the *Ars Amatoria*. When the marriage bond came to be more lightly respected and marriage often regarded only as a dynastic alliance, women found a compensation in the loose moral atmosphere of the time by encouraging lovers; and there were plenty of men ready to relax in the arms of a mistress. The loose relations between the sexes among the higher classes of society was one of the most obvious consequences of the disintegration, and one to which Augustus particularly addressed himself when he tried to bring about the moral regeneration of the city. We may respect the picture of Servilia taking command after the Ides of March; but it was not so respectable that Lucullus had to woo a mistress to obtain a command;[2] and Cicero's success in obtaining the consulship was in no small measure due to the babbling of

[1] The mother of M. Junius Brutus, one of Caesar's murderers.

[2] Plut. *Lucullus*, VI, 2 ff.

some young fool in his mistress' arms. The accomplished but unprincipled Sempronia is known to us from Sallust; Clodia has become a byword for loose morals. Praecia's power and the society which Sallust describes in his *Catilina* indicate a looseness in morals which found no compensating strictness in other spheres. The increasing freedom of women was a natural development, and had it taken place within an integrated society would have been a wholesome thing. But it was part of the general demoralization to surrender to the baser instincts, and too often it was women like Praecia or Clodia who wielded the influence, involving young men in their toils, leading them on to an extravagance beyond their means and to an acceptance of a moral code that was not good for Rome.

The lack of self-discipline was seen in the armies. Their ranks were increasingly filled from that class of people who possessed nothing, but hoped to make something for themselves from service in the army. Brought up as part of the rootless proletariat, they knew neither discipline nor loyalty. Many of the generals had few qualifications for their task except that they had bribed their way successfully to office at Rome; often they could not control their army; the army controlled them. The inglorious military careers of Fimbria and Flaccus, the cities offered for plunder, the treachery, the incitement of the army to turn against its general, all this showed the incompetence of the generals and the degree to which politics had entered the army. Since Sulla's appeal to his soldiers to march on Rome for *his* sake, this had become common;[1] Cinna made an impassioned plea to the army to fight on *his* behalf and save *his* position;[2] and Caesar was later to do the same. No Roman army was Roman; it belonged to a general. The indiscipline in Lucullus' army is known; in spite of his attempts to restore some measure of discipline, the army on occasions turned to booty rather than to duty, and eventually refused to move, thus leaving Mithridates to escape.

[1] Cf. also the oath which Sulla's soldiers swore in 83 B.C., Plut. *Sulla*, XXVII, 5.
[2] App. *Bell. Civ.* I, 65–6.

It is difficult to generalize about the army during this period, because we only hear of it when its behaviour brings it into prominence, although there must have been soldiers stationed in many of the provinces, such as Spain and Gaul, who carried out their duties quietly and without disobedience or disloyalty. But in the unsatisfactory state of the army organization, whereby every emergency required a special army raised under the recruiting system which had obtained since Marius, every army so raised consisted largely of men who were attracted by the reputation of the general and the sphere of war, in the hope of winning no small booty in the fighting and a piece of land on its conclusion. The soldiers felt an attachment to their general rather than to their country, and if he failed to attract their loyalty, then love of country did not fill the gap. If, on the other hand, the bond between the general and his men was close, it suited the purposes of the general to use their support for his own political ends, while it never seemed to the soldiers improper to allow themselves to become the tool of a general whose chief anxiety was his own political power and prestige. Hence the loyalty of the army depended almost entirely on the loyalty of their general; the Spanish armies were not tampered with and hence they caused no trouble; but Pompeius was able to regard Spain as his when the Civil War began, not merely because he had his personal lieutenants in command, but because his influence there was great; it was still a personal relationship, even though at that moment Pompeius stood for the government.

During these civil wars there was never an appeal to any ideal or principle, no cause to rally those who loved their country. Men attached themselves to the group with which they thought their interests coincided, or the one which seemed to hold out greater hopes. Only at the end of this disastrous period, when all men were weary of insensate civil war, was some ideal held before the people, the conflict of West against East; and then it could bring the whole of Italy together under the banner of Octavianus, and could give that positive surge which made possible not only

Actium but the Augustan Age itself. Romans had learnt again after a century to know the yearning of the spirit in its restless quest for its ideals.

It is worth while here to look at Caesar's defence of his action in marching against Rome; for in it we see the degree to which the individual had replaced the State in men's calculations. In the first book of the *Bellum Civile* he states his case in the way best suited to win sympathy and support. He admits that 'sibi semper primam fuisse dignitatem vitaque potiorem'.[1] His right to stand for the consulship *in absentia* had been taken from him; 'hanc iacturam honoris sui rei publicae causa aequo animo tulisse'.[2] His suggestion that all armies be disbanded had not been granted; levies were being held throughout Italy, the whole State was in arms; 'sed tamen ad omnia se descendere paratum atque omnia pati rei publicae causa'.[3] He then makes further suggestions for resolving the impasse. Again at Corfinium, he speaks to Lentulus Spinther, pointing out 'se non malefici causa ex provincia egressum sed uti se a contumeliis inimicorum defenderet... ut se et populum Romanum factione paucorum oppressum in libertatem vindicaret'.[4] And at Rome 'iniurias inimicorum commemorat...patientiam proponit suam, cum de exercitibus dimittendis ultro postulavisset, in quo iacturam dignitatis atque honoris ipse facturus esset. Acerbitatem inimicorum docet...iniuriam in eripiendis legionibus praedicat,[5] crudelitatem et insolentiam in circumscribendis tribunis plebis; condiciones a se latas, expetita colloquia et denegata commemorat'.[6]

I have made it clear above that Caesar had no choice; that the nobles had become selfish and corrupt, unfit to be Rome's governors; and that any man of ambition (and there should be scope for such men in a State) must oppose the nobles if he wished to achieve political success. Yet we are at first astonished when we

[1] *B.C.* I, 9, 2; cf. 7, 1 and 8.

[2] 9, 3.

[3] 9, 5.

[4] 22, 5.

[5] Note the quiet assumption that legions belong to generals, not to the State. Cf. Plut. *Cato Min.* XLV, 3.

[6] XXXII, 2 ff.

read Caesar's defence, both because of what he says, and because it is clear that these were the terms in which Caesar knew the people expected his defence to be argued. The whole burden of his case is that HIS *dignitas* and *existimatio* have been insulted; that he (an individual) has gone beyond what might be expected in offering concessions and compromises to the government; and that since the government will not listen to him, the preservation of his *dignitas* self-evidently requires that he lead his army against his country. The hostility of his *inimici* (political foes) leaves him no choice; it is he or they.

This was certainly true, but it does not alter the melancholy fact that this was the pass to which things had finally come; selfishness and lack of ideals, the concomitants of the disintegration, had ended finally in this, that the cause of the individual was the only one that counted. His attitude towards the Republic is amusing, were it not tragic; he is quite ready to be a dutiful member of the Republic, provided its government does what he says; otherwise the Republic is disloyal to Caesar. When he calls upon the rump of the Senate to help him govern the Republic, it is the Republic against which he has moved his armies because, as he naïvely explains, his *inimici* were trying to destroy him. We need not be surprised that armies gave their loyalty to individuals; here, at Rome's crisis, men were asked to give their loyalty to an individual.

This is the consummation of the development of decades, and shows that what happened in the armies was but in tune with what men did in every sphere, attached themselves to an individual or a group, because they had no country. Caesar's defence shows the contending parties driven to their last position: the individual on the side of the Populares, whose story was the story of a series of great, ambitious individuals; on the side of the nobles a powerful clique (the *inimici*) manipulating the machinery of government in their own interest, and determined to perpetuate the practice under the sacred name of the Republic. To them the Republic was a catchword; to Caesar it meant only a system of government. When he invited the Senate to join him in governing the Republic, he was, I am certain, sincere; the problem as he saw it was one of efficient government, and it seemed to him that it would be quite reasonable for himself, with the help of the Senate as a civil service, to govern the Republic without doing violence to the very idea of 'Republic'. For that we need not blame him; as an ideal the Republic was dead, except for a few men such as Cicero; he knew the facts, and what he planned did no injustice to the facts of the Republic. With Cicero the ideal of the Republic died, though Imperial discontents revived a sickly sentimental substitute, to which they gave all the virtues and qualities which seemed to them so lacking in their own government.

CHAPTER XIV

THE RELIGIOUS CONSEQUENCES

The spiritual disintegration was most clearly manifested in the realm of religion. In a harmonious society religion has two functions, one social and one individual. It is the cement which binds together the society, and its practice is public and communal. The effect of public worship upon the members of a community is very great; the individual feels himself strengthened in the company of others engaged in the same worship; there comes a sense not of less but of greater individuality when one is a fellow-member of a society which is one in the recognition of its God. There comes a self-confidence which strengthens the individual in his religious practice, when he feels that his personal God is also the God of all his fellow-members. For his religion remains personal and individual as well; men do not surrender their identity in public worship; rather do they find it, in the recognition of their own individual place in society. But when the harmony of the society is shattered, religion either disappears or becomes individual alone. Faith in the religion and the ideals of the society go hand in hand; when the first challenge to the ideals is issued, faith in the religion begins to waver, because they are so closely bound together, the ideals deriving their sanction from the religion.* The rationalism and questioning, whether of the Sophists or the nineteenth-century rationalists and political thinkers, was enough to destroy what they could not rebuild.

Much has been said of the formal nature of Roman religion even when it held a grip on Roman minds. It is suggested that it had not within it that quality which could make it a true religion; that its formality give it from the first something of the appearance of a business contract; and that its close connexion with politics later made it an instrument for political purposes, devoid of all religious content. This it certainly finally became; and the beginning has possibly been argued from the end. We must be careful; the form and formality of Roman religion were an expression of the Roman mind and spirit, and we must start from that fact. Because the Romans regarded their relations with Heaven rather in the light of an agreement, that does not mean that their attitude was not religious; it means only that, as they saw their human relations in that way, they fashioned their relations with the objects of their religious instinct according to a similar pattern. We cannot infer that the strength or depth of their religious feeling was less than that of other people's. That the Romans of the second century were religious I have argued above; and in the middle of that century Panaetius was making it possible for educated Romans to continue their belief in their religion, by combining the best of the old Roman tradition with the Stoic conception of the Universe and man's place and duty in it, a process which was necessary in view of Rome's new responsibility towards the world. It could have made possible a continuing faith in their destiny and their traditional values, while adding that clear conception of a mission which in fact did not come till Augustus.

The political crisis destroyed that hope. In the struggle that followed upon the Gracchan experiment, the Senate's opponents began to attack the hitherto accepted values of their society; sneers and jeers at privilege and wealth, the contrast of their own untutored genius denied an outlet, became the means whereby their opponents sought to discredit the nobles' standing, suggesting that privilege and exclusiveness were their only claim to govern.* The high ideals they had set before themselves, their sense of duty and responsibility went unnoticed by those whose ambitions never aspired beyond the winning of power and the breaking of their exclusiveness. It had been exclusive, but it had not for that reason been a sham; it had been believed in and had been their moral guide in the conduct of their responsibilities. But it necessarily followed that they would safeguard their position if they could, and thus thrown on the defensive they fought with what arms they could in defence of their privileges, not their code.*

Their code and values having been attacked, their religious faith was necessarily shaken too. Here Rome was unfortunate. Religion and political life had always been closely associated; no action was taken, no move made, no legislation enacted unless the favour of Heaven had first been ascertained. Religion could therefore easily become the tool of politics; and when it began to lose a hold upon their spirit, it was quickly enlisted to keep a grip on the political machine. At the end of the second century the election to priestly offices was made a political issue by those who hoped to break the nobles' control of priestly politics and to exercise it in their own interest.* Thus brought openly into the political arena it could not hope to survive as a spiritual force. We need not describe the depths to which Roman religion was dragged in the fight for power; the years 60–50 B.C. provide abundant illustration of the final catastrophe to the religion, when all parties regarded religion as a trump card which could beat all other knavish tricks in politics. It was a convention which all accepted; if a religious impediment could be found, it was sufficient to balk a piece of legislation, keep a candidate out of office or postpone an election. Only once did it fail, in 59 B.C., when Caesar would not agree to trumps.*

Religion, then, as a function of society, was dead at Rome. Individuals there were still who seem to have believed in the gods of Rome and worshipped at their shrines; but to most Jupiter was too heavily involved in politics to command their religious respect. They turned to other, less compromised, deities. Men and women of many nations and creeds who had come to Rome as slaves had brought with them their own gods, and in the course of time these struck root in Rome in spite of official disapproval.

These Eastern religions were non-Roman in their spirit and appeal, and in earlier days the Senate had successfully opposed their entry. But when slaves became freedmen and citizens, when Roman armies came into contact with the countries of their origin, it became impossible to impose a ban, even if men would.

Sometimes they made the effort; four times between 58 and 48 B.C. were the shrines of Isis destroyed, and four times rebuilt. So long as Rome had no religion of her own, they could not hope to destroy the religious urge in men by forbidding that which gave it satisfaction. Yet for Rome the flourishing of alien religions in her midst spelt danger. For when religion is individual alone, should there be a conflict between religion and society, religion will always win, since it is that in which a man believes even to the point of death; in crises it is that for which he will fight, even if need be, against society. The Roman Empire was to discover that simple truth when it capitulated to Christianity.

But these Eastern religions had not in the atmosphere of Rome that social quality which alone could have made their presence welcome. They were religions of salvation, in which the devotee was shown the way to personal salvation through some prescription independent of society. Their main attraction at this time was for the lower classes, those unhappy men and women who were in but not of society, poorer people who could not feel themselves a part of their society; and in the ensuing loneliness of spirit they turned to those religions which by their very mysteries and initiation gave their devotees a sense of membership of a society and a feeling of anchorage which they could not feel in their mundane relations. The promise of happiness now and eternal bliss in the hereafter brought to the restless spirits of those who enjoyed neither privilege nor security something with which a political Jupiter could never hope to compete.* Their appeal was to the same classes of people who later turned to early Christianity for spiritual help and companionship amid the desolation of their environment. They formed their own society, but it was not Rome's.

There was a further significance. In times of unhappiness and uncertainty men, when they live together though they are not a society, without the anchorage which the code of a healthy society provides, are liable to proceed to excesses and exaggerations which have no place in a healthy society. The coldly formal worship of Rome in its healthy days could not be adequate for many at this time.* In proportion as man finds himself alone and unsupported by society, he becomes more desperate in his attempts to join himself to his God. At first, when times are fat and easy, he gives himself to bodily and material pleasure; but when uncertainty and tribulation come, many become aware of their loneliness, fear and uncertainty urge them on to unhealthy extremes, and they seek the solace of some orgiastic worship, where, by working themselves into a frenzied state, they can persuade themselves that they are becoming one with their God. Many of these Eastern religions had in them an orgiastic element; and their increasing popularity was in no small measure due to the elements of mystery and mysticism combined with an orgiastic ritual.

Similarly the occult became popular. In uncertain times men tend to be attracted to the mystical and the occult, in their effort to know the future when the future may hold so many ills; means to penetrate the darkness of the future were eagerly sought. Soothsayers and prophets became not uncommon; Nigidius Figulus attained to fame by his ability to cast a horoscope; the art of astrology was cultivated; and omens and portents were seen and interpreted. Whether the future could be foretold became a subject for discussion; Stoicism under Poseidonius added the great weight of its reputation in favour of the future's predictability. These gropings after answers were a sign that men were worried what the future held; and such anxiety only comes when it is all too likely that the future has bad news, when the sure hope of a confident society has been dissolved in the nagging uncertainty which is the companion of disintegration.

The Eastern religions were on the whole the refuge of the foreign-born and less educated elements at Rome. The educated classes, when they felt the need for refuge, found it generally in philosophy. The two systems which attracted most Romans were the Epicurean and the Stoic, both of which had been born in the days when the city-states of Greece had fallen before the Macedonian monarchy. Epicureanism had accepted the new conditions and advocated a way of life in conformity with the loss of political liberty and the opportunities of political activity. To withdraw from public life to a serene unruffled seclusion, avoiding excess in order to escape the pain when balance was established, was the life to which it exhorted men to aspire. It was the peaceful quiet of the weak and the disgusted. Such a philosophy must necessarily have an appeal at Rome in the days of its disintegration, when dishonesty and corruption were all around; to avoid the pitfalls of public life was common sense to men like Atticus, who behind this shield could keep the friendship of all parties. They could seem to justify their abstention from public life, and Lucretius could thunder at those who were wracked by the tortures of thwarted ambition and the strain of the political battle. But was the answer to withdraw? For all they did was to retire behind the structure of society into their selfish seclusion, leaving to others the task of maintaining that structure whose collapse would involve all equally.* It was a selfish, anti-social philosophy, such as could flourish only in a distempered society; its precepts had been looked upon with odium in the second century, when individual and society were at one. While it might give comfort to many who were unhappy in the society of their day, neither from it nor from them could come that moral regeneration of which Rome stood in such sore need.*

But if it could not be a source for positive good, it certainly could for positive ill. For while the 'pleasure' of its founder was innocent enough, any scheme of conduct which put personal pleasure as the final end of man was capable of distortion and travesty. In this age when moral standards had deteriorated, when the ideals of society had given way to selfish materialism, such a philosophy could easily be twisted to seem to give a sanction to all and every pleasure of the body; and behind the screen of seeming-fair philosophy man might indulge his every whim. This too happened of necessity; and Epicureanism came to include within its fold the coarse sensualist together with the timid and the disgusted.

If Epicureanism could not become the basis of a moral code for society, Stoicism could. It had been in the earlier years, and for a time was to assume that role again in the Empire; and there were during this period many Stoics of high character. But it failed now, as it was to fail under the Empire, because of itself it was not enough. A philosophy cannot do duty for a religion; it may help a man to lead a blameless life; it cannot unaided weld a harmonious society out of its individuals. It lacks that quality of inspiration that belongs to religion, which comes from conceiving one's aims and duties as having a sanction outside one's society, involving a personal relationship with that power. Religion requires faith, philosophy reason; and reason never made or kept together a society. The ethical code of Stoicism, with its emphasis on duty, the cosmopolitanism of its conception of God, when conjoined to the Roman faith, could broaden and interpret that faith; but as a code of life it had a certain fatalistic quality, teaching one to accept one's destiny, which was fated whether one agreed or not; it could help a man to do his duty and die well; it could not vivify society. The idea of Fatum, when combined with the religious instinct of Virgil, could produce a magnificent religious statement of Rome's destiny; without it it showed only the way to a noble death.

The influence of Stoicism under Panaetius had been great and good in the second century, and its products continued to give a moral leadership into the first century. But they were its products when society was harmonious; the next generation could not show its counterpart to Rutilius Rufus or Scaevola, not because Stoicism had changed, but because society had, and though there were still good Stoics made, they could no longer exercise the same influence on society nor identify their Stoicism with their Rome. The writings of Cicero and Varro, the great influence of Poseidonius and Antiochus, alike bear witness to the widespread interest in philosophy among educated men; the corruption, hooliganism and cheating in public life bear witness to the inability of these men to influence their fellows or their morals. Both Varro and Cicero were aware of some lack in Roman life;

Varro employed his qualities of genius and research in an attempt to revive the Roman religion by writing a detailed account of its gods and practices, in the hope that men would read and fall in love. Cicero's praise of Varro's efforts agrees with his general attitude towards the *di patrii*, belief in whom he held to be fundamental to the welfare of the State.* Yet both were aware that things were not as they should be; Varro contrasts the present with the better past, and even with his own early days; Cicero's imaginative life is lived in the circle of Scipio, when Roman society seemed to him to be at its best and happiest; both feel a restless, spiritual disquiet, whose origin they cannot precisely determine, and whose cure they feel instinctively is to be found in the religious regeneration of society.

CHAPTER XV

THE ITALIAN COUNTRYSIDE

All that we have said in this description of the Roman disintegration refers to the city of Rome. It is our misfortune that the Italian countryside produced no literature of its own, and that we are therefore confronted with an unsurmountable obstacle when we try to evaluate the spiritual condition of the small country towns, and to estimate the extent to which we can predicate of them what we have predicated of Rome. Yet it is of the greatest importance for our purpose that we should form some estimate, in order that our perspective may not be distorted.

We may start from the assumption that the countryside is always more conservative than the city, and that intellectual movements, fashions, and social conventions always take time to permeate the countryside, if they ever do.[1] This is particularly so where communications tend to give a semi-independence to the country; and in first-century Italy, although the military roads represented as fine a system of communication as the ancient world offered, yet it remains true that travel was slow and dangerous. The journey to Naples would normally take two days; we can therefore see that the country towns in Northern and Central Italy stood at a considerable distance from Rome by their reckoning. Further, the escaped slaves and brigands who infested the highways made a journey a hazardous adventure which few would venture upon without a protective suite; and this most country-dwellers would not be able to afford. We may, then, reasonably surmise that the countryside and towns lived lives largely untouched by the spiritual and intellectual currents of

[1] I am referring to the countryside before wireless, television and fast and safe communication brought country people into much closer contact with the city.

Rome; and that while the wealthier citizens might make occasional visits to Rome because of the attractions and novelties of the large city, and its importance for business purposes, yet they neither subscribed to nor were influenced by its spiritual and moral tone; and that though wealthy Roman citizens and magistrates might spend some time in these towns, yet their influence on the community would be negligible.

There is therefore good reason to suppose that country life would be almost wholly unaffected by Rome's moral standards, unless the same causes that operated at Rome to bring about the disintegration were at work also in the countryside. But were they? We have seen that the distemper began in the political sphere, and worked out from there as the fight absorbed more and more of their energies, forced them to ever lower depths, and split Rome into contending factions which claimed all their members' loyalty. Now this political battle, important though it was, was centred in Rome, and in the absence of representative elections, hardly passed beyond the *pomerium*. If ambitious men in the country aspired to a political career, they went to Rome; who was to be consul, who to govern Asia, were problems which left the countryside unruffled; those who chose to be ruffled left their country town and made for Rome. The political battle therefore was local to Rome. Again, the provinces felt the consequences both because they received governors from Rome, were the victims of their and the Equites' financial greed, and not infrequently the scene of a military success; Italy was free of this.

Their distance from Rome and their political status protected them from direct contact with the source of the disintegration; and we know of no cause which would work a similar mischief independently of Rome. On the other hand such miserable evidence as we have suggests that what we might under these circumstances expect in these communities was in fact to be found. It is clear from the occasional descriptions in Cicero's speeches where country clients are involved that country towns were close-knit communities, inspired with a strong sense of loyalty. Their sons, if they went to Rome in pursuit of a career, seem to have felt that their success was a source of honour to the town of their origin, the local citizens seem to have followed with anxious interest the careers of those who went to Rome, and to have joined with them in rejoicing at their success.* The pride of Cicero himself in his native Arpinum is witness to this; he was proud of Marius' great achievements, proud too that he himself had brought it further signal honour.

Consonant with this picture of a live society is the vitality of its religion which we seem to observe. Here again we should expect this devotion to a religion which had lost its force at Rome, unless there were some destroying cause; and we know none. If the countryside in later centuries could for so long withstand the onset of Christianity in its devotion to its own small gods, we should need some strong, compelling reason to explain its temporary eclipse at this time. Simple religious faith and old-time customs strike deep roots in the countryside; and when small towns remained comparatively unchanged for generations, not suddenly engulfed by vast industrial changes or economic developments, we should expect there too what we have seen in the countryside of England and Europe. And this seems to have been the case. Virgil's deep religious feelings and his love of the countryside are the products of the country; the poet who could write 'Fortunatus et ille deos qui novit agrestes'[1] must have known those *di agrestes* and not been alone in his knowledge. Both he and Tibullus are witnesses to the liveliness of the simple religion of the country, which continued untainted and untarnished by the rottenness of Rome. Livy too with his deep understanding of the true grandeur of Rome and his religious faith in her destiny, was country born and bred; Cicero's belief in Rome and her *di patrii*, in the solidity of the true Roman character, was the product of his upbringing at Arpinum, where these things were still true, as he had hoped they were at Rome. When he turns to the second century B.C. for his

[1] *Georgics*, II, 493.

ideal Rome, he is turning to that period in which Rome's society seemed to him to conform to the standards he knew in his small country town; his zeal to make the Romans Roman explains his disappointment at his failure; he could not realize that he was talking at Rome in terms they could not understand, referring to values they could not comprehend, and exhorting them to a virtue they despised and did not want.

This, if it is true, puts a different emphasis on the Augustan regeneration. The Augustan revolution represented the conquest by the politically unrepresented Italians over the selfish political power-holders of Rome;[1] it went further. The spiritual and moral reformation at which Augustus aimed represented the attempt by the countryside and towns to conquer Rome in that province too; it was the counterpart to the political victory, and was perhaps the more important part. Rome had failed her Empire; of that there could be no doubt. Large parts of Italy had had to fight for political equality, and having won their cause of equal privilege, had withdrawn again into their own life. There can have been no great love engendered by the Social War; and even though resentment might have smouldered and died down, no fire of loyalty and love had yet been lit.* The simpler dwellers of the country would have feared the city's evil influence; those who went to Rome would have learnt, like Cicero, to know its hollow sham, its corruption and its betrayal of its own great past. When the countrymen took possession of the city, they set to cleaning up its morals, restoring to it its religion which they had kept alive, reviving the sanctity of family life, as it was in the country, and as it had been once at Rome. Virgil, Livy, Horace, Tibullus, Augustus himself were all non-Roman in this sense; Rome's destiny was seen through the eyes of countrymen, not Romans; and it was the countrymen's moral code and religious spirit which Augustus sought to introduce to Rome. Thus should his attempt

[1] See Sherwin White, *The Roman Citizenship*, 147–8; and his reference to Rudolph, *Stadt und Staat im römischen Italien*, 219; Syme, *The Roman Revolution*, 82–94, 363–5.

be understood; it would have been childish to attempt to put the clock back to the 'good old days'; it was only because these things were present and living forces outside Rome that he felt they could be imposed in Rome. Ovid's and Julia's circles showed that he could only succeed in part; a large city can never behave as a country town; but nevertheless the countryside did save Rome's soul and allow her to fulfil her mission.*

CHAPTER XVI

LITERATURE AND THOUGHT

Literature had reached a turning-point; it was no longer sufficient to produce something as nearly as possible the equal of a Greek original; the language was now sufficiently developed, the individual sufficiently aware of himself as well as of his society, and society sufficiently mature for some form of literary expression which could belong to the individual as part of society. In the *Satires* of Lucilius this had been found, and what he created became a unique Roman contribution to Western literature. The combined influence of Stoicism and Alexandrian scholarship created a lively interest in scholarly and philological studies; Lucilius and Accius both occupied themselves with matters philological and orthographical; now was laid the foundation of that literary Latin which effectively swamped vulgar Latin for centuries; the beginnings of Rome's greatest single contribution to the Western world, namely jurisprudence, were now made. But none of this was literature; and indeed this period is barren of performance. This was in part due to the changed political atmosphere, in part also to the need to find something to express and some medium through which to express it.

Politically the Scipionic serenity had been sadly disturbed by the Gracchi; nor did the political events connected with the Jugurthine War allow a return to calm; affairs tended to take precedence over letters among the class best able to practise them, the educated class of nobles. Further, this was the period when Rome's relations with the Italians became increasingly strained; in the growing political animosity Rome was cutting herself off from those to whom her literature already owed much and was to owe more. In the subtly changed atmosphere of the post-Gracchan period the destruction of the nobles' self-assurance destroyed also that unruffled equanimity which had made possible the interests of the Scipionic circle. It had been possible then to brood upon philosophical problems without feeling any clamant insistence to deal with some particular problem lest disaster follow. The problems were more urgent now and to these they perforce applied themselves.

Apart from the inimical atmosphere, what were they to express, and how? The earlier decision to give themselves wholly to the production of literature along Greek lines and thus found a Roman literature which was Greek in form and partly also in spirit, had caused to be almost completely atrophied any native forms of self-expression which might have developed and become an appropriate vehicle for what a Roman might think fit to reveal of himself. Committed as they were to Greece, they must look there once more, and once again they would feel the difference between the Greek and Roman spirit. The Roman upbringing, its *mos maiorum*, the insistence on public service, and the practical and particular bent of their thinking would prevent a Roman from revealing the secrets of his heart in the lyric forms of Greece; their interests would remain centred on the State, though in keeping with the discordance of the times their literature would tend to be partisan and aggressive or self-defensive; and what they wrote would be likely to reflect the tensions and the animosities which were distracting the state to its destruction. Literature would be less confined within the aristocracy; others would join the battle of words which was part of the political battle in the last decades of the Republic; once again men from Italy would make their contribution to Roman letters, less fettered by the *mos maiorum* and the Roman character, but equally in thrall to the spirit of disintegration.

One form of literature which became common as the century wore on and which owed its spirit to the times was that of memoir and biography; it was the product of the emerging individualism which we have noted and of the changed political conditions. As attacks on individuals became common, attacks which involved the integrity and the policy of certain men, the need was felt to state one's case, to put one's point of view and return the attack upon one's opponents. The courts were no longer sufficient; their justice was too often tempered by narrow considerations of politics, nor would a speech of defence reach the ears of those who had heard from the tribune's platform the bitter and sometimes unfounded allegations of those whose aim was power, not truth. The written word acquired greater importance during this century; books reached a wider and more varied audience, epigrams were posted up and strewn about the city, as politics became the occupation and the sport of so many people. Aemilius Scaurus, Lutatius Catulus, Rutilius Rufus, all of whom had been victims of important political attacks involving more than their own good names, began a practice which became frequent in the next years. Sulla and Caesar wrote their memoirs; Pompeius' biography was written; we hear of attacks by the elder Curio on Caesar, of the *Trikaranos* of Varro, of Catos and anti-Catos, of writings by Lucullus; and the list could be extended. All served a political purpose, and were the offspring of the individualism and the political life of the times.

In poetry Lutatius Catulus and his circle inaugurated a new age. Catulus, retired from active political life, became the centre of a circle interested in poetry and literature, which enthusiastically studied the contemporary Greek works of Alexandria. This was in itself significant; Alexandrian literature had not in the second century deeply influenced Rome, which had preferred instinctively the earlier literature of Greece. Hellenistic literature was the self-conscious product of a people for whom the State no longer existed; the Greek spirit had felt the change and both in literature and philosophy turned in upon itself; both became personal, individual concerns, and literature became an artificial product ruled by self-imposed canons of the study. When Romans began to be interested in this poetry, their society too was beginning to lose its attractive force on men's loyalty; and as the Alexandrians held in high esteem the lyric poets of early Greece, themselves the products of their disintegrating times, so were both the Alexandrians and lyricists to come into favour in Rome's similar time of stress.

What Catulus and his friends wrote was not in itself of any great value; its value lay rather in the interest it engendered in this new form of literature, which was to have so fine a flowering with Catullus. But we may discern in what they wrote how unsuited to the Roman character and temperament was this form of literature; their poems were careful imitations of Greek poems on Greek themes; they addressed a lover or a favourite because that was what the Greek epigram did; there is no sparkle of life or originality, though evidence enough of ingenuity and care; and for that reason they were valuable. Their efforts laid the foundations for those who could by temperament build upon them; to a Roman a love epigram or lyric was quite alien, and only to be indulged as an interesting exercise. Though they had turned by instinct to Alexandria, their Roman background forbade them to make these works their own, and they failed to capture its spirit and translate it into Roman terms.

The *neoteroi* were the successful exponents of the new literary forms with which Catulus and his circle had familiarized Rome. Of all they wrote we have only the works of Catullus, the greatest of them; but we know sufficient of the rest to be able to form some judgement of their aims and ideals. At the time they reached maturity, the disintegration had gone far; it was not long before Caesar's army would cross the Rubicon to mark the Republic's death. They were all young, and knew nothing of the calmer, stabler days of the last century; to them Rome was the corrupt, pleasure-seeking, loose, immoral but none the less exciting and stimulating capital of an Empire of whose mission and responsibilities they had no understanding or concern; an infinitely more diverting and delightful place than Northern Italy could show. Their youth absorbed its pleasures and unhappiness, and brilliantly reflected them. To them the past was stuffy; they did not understand the true *gravitas* of older Rome, and regarded what they mistook for it in present Rome as starchy arrogance at which they put out their tongues. They had not the age or understanding to feel that things were out of joint; this would have come with time, but fate denied them that alone; and so they remained their age's brilliant mirror.

The individualism of Alexandria attracted them, for they too were individualists. They were true disciples of Callimachus in believing that μέγα βιβλίον, μέγα κακόν; not for them the epic, but the epyllion, the epigram, the lyric; Ennius was rough and antiquated, not suited to their age; Alexandria with its short, artificial and meticulously laboured poems was the object of their admiration and the first source of their inspiration. They laboured at epyllia for their own satisfaction, living for themselves, and indifferent to the criticisms of others so long as what they wrote conformed to their standards and won their circle's applause. They taught Rome to pay due heed to care in composition; *ingenium* without *ars* would never more win Roman approbation; but the 'Smyrna', had it been preserved, would have shown us only Rome's unhealthy moral tone and her failure to provide inspiration and ideals for poets. The 'Lock of Berenice' and the 'Peleus and Thetis' are excellently done; but they are wholly unrelated to Rome or her society, and draw their inspiration not even from Alexandria but from Alexandrian poems. The 'Lock of Berenice' is in much the same class as a copy of verses for the Porson Prize; the 'Peleus and Thetis' is not much different; there is no attempt to reinterpret the story or use it as a vehicle for the poet's own message; *ars* predominates; a successful exercise in a new technique.

In his shorter poems Catullus is more successful as a poet, because he is himself. True, he borrows and experiments with fresh forms and metres; but what he says is his own, the emotions he expresses are his, the pathos and the wit spontaneous and his. The individual has come into his own, and he does not shrink from revealing himself; he vents his spleen on those he does not like, shows his lack of interest in affairs of State, though not in politicians; and feels no self-consciousness to reveal the sorrow and the torture of his soul. It is quite un-Roman, and in Latin poetry quite unique; only the conjunction of circumstances made it possible, the young North Italian coming to a Rome that excited but did not shape, at a time when the *ethos* of society was lost amid the petty selfishness of wrangling foes and the moral laxness that had followed. Saved by his birth from the restraints which held back Romans, he was able to be himself and know no curbing influence other than the technical ones of his own making. He is one of the great individualists of his time, the Caesar of literature;[1] both snapped their fingers at conventions when they would; both determined that the established order, whether of state or literature, must conform to them; nay, they would both inaugurate the new established order, sweeping away the cobwebs of the dreary past, remodelling, renewing and themselves dictating.

Alike in so much they were alike in failure. Caesar, for all his great success, was doomed to fail and die for his success; his form of government was not the form that Romans finally adopted; in his Rome he could achieve a temporary success; but that was due to the disjointed times. When Romans came to themselves once more, it was not to accept his efficient form of government, but one that seemed at least to be more like the form he had despised;[2] the *res publica restituta*,[3] much though it owed to Caesar, was the epitaph that told his failure. So also with Catullus; Latin letters owed much to him and his contemporaries, and their lesson of thoroughness and care was not forgotten; but the Augustan Age could not approve of what he wrote. Rome was again a society, conscious of a mission; Virgil and Horace, though they had drunk at Alexandria's wells, as times grew settled found that water bitter; Virgil turned to Ennius, whom the *neoteroi* despised, for inspiration to produce an epic, which they had thought bad taste and tedious. Horace makes lyric Roman; no more un-Roman

[1] I am thinking of Caesar as a political figure.

[2] Cf. Suetonius, *Iulius*, 77: nihil esse rem publicam; appellationem modo, sine corpore ac specie.

[3] Of Augustus, a theme which he emphasized on coins and elsewhere.

outbursts of the bitter heart; no more crude or vulgar poems;* only what became a Roman to declare would Horace say; he would speak with all the Roman pride of Roman *virtus* and condemn the very circles which had nourished Catullus. He did not approve of the *neoteroi*; his *Odes* were Catullus' *res publica restituta*.

Never again, as never before, did Romans reveal to the world the poignant sorrows of the heart; Catullus and Caesar stand together as the great individuals who in Rome's time of trouble tried to trample on her deepest feelings, only to find that Rome was greater than they. It was for this reason that Cicero remarked that were his life twice as long, he still would not have time to read lyric poets.[1] For Cicero felt the true greatness of the Roman character; he was in conflict with the Rome of his day, seeking his inspiration in what he deemed the glorious days of Scipio, when men thought of State not self, and did not set themselves above the State, nor claim allegiance to themselves. The *neoteroi* chose to despise that past, and found their interest in themselves and their environment; they were part of the life that Cicero thought rotten, and in it they took their pleasure. It was impossible that Cicero should look with favour and applaud such men; he opposed Catullus as he opposed Caesar, because both opposed the spirit of the Republic. Between him and them there could be finally no compromise; and Imperial Rome agreed with Cicero.

The historian reflects most clearly his society, both in what he writes and how he writes it. Whether his theme be his society or that of others, whether contemporary or past, it will express the aims and ideals, the problems and the criticisms current at the time. What seems important, what irrelevant in history is shown us; a history of their own society reveals their attitude towards their past and present, their hopes, if any, for the future; we may see whether the present overwhelms their understanding of the past, whether present discontents force them to defend their case through history, or whether their assurance in the present and the

[1] Seneca, *Epist.* XLIX, 5.

future gives them a balanced view and full of faith; Gibbon in this way tells us as much of his society as Macaulay does of his. Sallust, Livy and Tacitus show us the temper of their times; Sallust reveals the bitterness of the political battle, the feeling that things are ill that must be rightened; Livy the faith and confidence in Rome, in her great past and greater future; Tacitus the fatalistic acquiescence in a form of government, sometimes better, sometimes worse, which in any case no man could master, and to which all men must bow. All of them sum up the spirit of their different ages.

Sallust's works represent the bloom of history of this age. He had taken his part in political life, and seems to have been no better and no worse than many others; but his opponents were able to drive him from political life, and thus turned him to Caesar as his and the Republic's hope. He had tasted the bitter disappointment of politics, saw the absence of responsibility and ideals, recognized as empty catchwords the constitutional cries which all men raised to conceal the facts of selfish striving for power and wealth. By this time the State had reached its final crisis; neither side was sincere, neither the nobles who asserted the claims of the constitution and the Republic, nor their opponents who proposed mischievous legislation and stirred up the basest instincts of the mob in the sacred name of *libertas* and the Republic.

He was right in what he thought he saw, but his disillusioned cynicism and pessimism forbade him to see the good in one particular man, namely Cicero. He could not understand Cicero's position or the motives that led him in his policy. To Sallust Cicero was a *novus homo*, whose ambition was to climb the social ladder and associate with the nobles. This was not wholly wrong, but he missed the true motive force of Cicero's behaviour; Cicero, brought up in the purer air of Arpinum, respecting Rome's great traditions, her *virtus* and her *mos maiorum*, disappointed though he was to find them unknown or looked on slightingly in Rome, was trying none the less to recall his Rome to her own great standards of the past. He respected the ideals of the Republic with a love and awe that to Sallust must have marked him for a simple countryman unacquainted with the city; while those who lived at Rome knew the truth. Cicero's aim was to restore the harmony which was no longer there; significantly, *concordia* was the basis of his aims and hopes; the nobles must still be Rome's true governors, who must be accepted and respected. He knew their imperfections; how accurately he had measured them we cannot precisely say; his state of mind lent itself to self-deception. He wanted them to be good, therefore they must be capable of goodness; therefore they were not irredeemably bad; a simple piece of self-deception, if it is.

But Cicero's admiration for the nobles as a class Sallust mistook for admiration of the individuals, some of whom he held responsible for his political disgrace, most of whom he thought were unworthy of their claims; to Sallust therefore Cicero was doubly contemptible, for he was trying to be what he was not, and what in any case it was shame to want to be. And for these same reasons he found in Caesar the object of his admiration. Caesar was an individualist; in Sallust's eyes he stood out above all parties and disputes, imposing his will on both sides, in thrall to neither, bending events and people to his wishes, never swayed by others. This, so it seemed to Sallust, was the man to restore the Republic to its former greatness, to banish from it all that had brought it to its present degradation, to inform it with his will and purpose, and to set it on the road to future greatness. For Sallust loved the Republic no less than Cicero; he too thought he saw wherein it had come to fail and how it could be set aright.

He was wholly wrapped in the present and concerned for the distempers of the time. To him the problem was a moral one, with greed, selfishness, extravagance, immorality as the causes; to a degree he was right; but he failed to see that they were also results; the subtle interconnexion of cause and effect escaped him, that though bad morals were undoubtedly breeding their like, yet there must be some reason for the rotten parentage. Sallust hoped by stamping out these vices to purify society; he did not see that, as in the parable, they must be replaced by virtues, and men will not be virtuous to order, but only by conviction. Legislation and suppression could not cleanse society, only a change of heart and will. And as long as the internecine strife continued, both sides would be driven to all extremes, and every corner of life would feel the effects of the enforced bad conduct of the Forum.

Unable to get beyond his own experience, he saw the cheating and chicanery of public life and asked himself how it had come to be. He turned his mind towards the past,* and found in the Jugurthine War what he wanted. The nobles were responsible, and then their monopoly of government and their dishonesty were first challenged. He had prejudged the question when he set out to search; it seemed to him that the nobles should have set the good example, not the bad; and since they had had the prerogative in the earlier days, they must have been the class responsible. The events of the Jugurthine War lent themselves to partisan interpretation; then it was that a *novus homo*, supported by the Equites, had first successfully opposed the ruling class; in the animosity of the moment accusations of corruption and treachery had been freely hurled, and those who opposed their wishes or stood in their way had been brought to task. To Sallust there was no doubt who was wrong; his imagination created the nobles in the image of their grandsons, and Marius in the image of Caesar; all that he saw in the nobles of his time he projected on to their grandfathers; and Marius stood out with Caesar's rugged independence. It seemed, then, to him that the nobles had begun the scheming, the bribery, the subordination of the State's best interests to their own, and even if they had not begun it then, it was then that it was first exposed and challenged. How this degeneration of the nobles had come about he explains in none but the most general moral terms;* for the rest, it was sufficient to talk of their pride and exclusiveness, contemptuous of the outsider, inconsiderate of Rome; from this beginning all had flowed; let but this insolence be checked and all men be virtuous perforce, and Rome would be saved; and Caesar alone could do it.

The corruption had continued, and so does Sallust's interpretation of Roman history. He hated Sulla, for Sulla had restored the *dominatio* of the nobles. The merits of Sulla's attempt to remedy the State escaped his embittered notice; unlike Sulla he could not see wherein lay the true cause of Rome's disaster, and to him Sulla was eternally damned because through him the nobles breathed again. His *Histories* are his interpretation of the events that followed Sulla's death, his theme the nobles' failure to rise to responsibility, and the bitterness engendered between them and those from whom political rights had been wrongfully snatched. He sees that by now neither side is right, but the gravamen of the blame he puts with those whose opportunities and hence responsibilities were greater.

In the *Catilina* he has chosen a theme which will allow him to portray the social and moral disintegration of his own time, and he does it well. His description is incisive, his interpretation less so. It was his own experience of these conditions which set him to explain their cause, and his explanation is a moral one. He does not realize the extent to which the conditions of the time served to perpetuate the low moral standards, making it all but impossible for individual or group to eschew improper behaviour without suffering annihilation; he is quite certain that the moral decline must have begun in the moral sphere; men had been originally simple and virtuous; then had come wealth, luxury and ambition with all the vices in their train, ousting virtue from society. His concern for youth is great; brought up into the society of Rome with bad examples round them, seeing the behaviour of their elders, they became like all around them, and so the evil sprouted further evil. The utter failure of the system he did not appreciate; nor did he understand that when a State has come to the pass to which Rome had come, no moral legislation could save her, only the hand of someone stronger than them all, who could end the political fight, give society back its ideals and allow men to lead moral lives in, not out of, society. As things were both sides must fight with every weapon at their disposal, or confess defeat; and neither side was prepared for that.

Yet, if we may accept as genuine his *Letters to Caesar*,* he was finally driven, like Cicero, to advocate that some strong man should take upon himself to cleanse society, and having accomplished this, withdraw. Caesar he cast for this role, hoping that he would exercise a power similar to Sulla's, but for better purposes. Unlike Cicero he thought that once life had been purified Caesar could retire, while life continued at its higher level.[1] Cicero too realized the need for some controlling hand, but hoped that such a hand could exercise its power without damage to the Republic; that the *auctoritas* of some pre-eminent citizen would suffice to keep in restraint the passions and excesses of his fellows; instinctively he knew that the controlling hand must hover always over Rome, that affairs would not go well unless someone was ever there to intervene.[2] Both were true lovers of the Republic, both had realized that some superior power was needed; neither could be expected to see that in that fact was concealed the Republic's death. Sallust, consumed by the present, thought of Sulla; Cicero, steeped in the past, turned his hopes to Scipio; the answer was to lie in a subtle combination of the two.

The style of Sallust further reflects the age as well as the man. It was an age of battling styles, when what they had no longer satisfied, but their restlessness, knowing not its cause, could not devise the answer; the result was a groping alike in style and form after they knew not what, because they were discontented with the present. Sallust's style is the outcome of his moral interpretation of Roman events; he passed his moral judgement on the present, tracing the first cause of Rome's downfall to the destruction of Carthage[3] and the ensuing freedom from fear and the growing luxury; before that fatal date Rome had been healthy, and the elder Cato seemed to embody what Sallust admired in the preceding years.* His strong moral views, his uncompromising hostility to peccant nobles, the simple forthrightness with which

[1] See Calevo, *Il problema della tendenziosità di Sallustio*, 20 ff.
[2] I am referring to the views set forth in the *De Re Publica*.
[3] *Cat.* x, 1; *Hist.* frag. 11 (Maurenbrecher).

he expressed his views, all in Sallust's eyes stood forth as a beacon amid the moral darkness of his own day, and the rotund effeminacy of the modern style. He thought he shared Cato's outlook, and he decided to share to some extent his style and vocabulary. It was, I think, this combination of admiration and sympathy with the Cato of his imagination which induced him to put himself in literary indebtedness to him.*

Similarly with Thucydides. Sallust was not setting out to write a descriptive history of his times, but an analytical history to show how Rome had reached her present pass. It did not seem to him that the causes lay on the surface, but deep down at the very roots of human nature; the reason was to be found in the appetites of men unrestrained by reason or scruple. In Thucydides he saw an analyst whose deep insight into the truth of things had cut away the irrelevant to reveal the Peloponnesian War and what had happened in it as the ineluctable results of human nature in certain circumstances; he had used the Peloponnesian War as the medium through which to illustrate the working of human nature in society; and for that reason he could claim that his history would be useful to future generations because what he described was likely to happen again in much the same way.

Thucydides had written a universal history out of a particular war, and he had succeeded by standing aside and viewing events from the vantage point of an impartial observer contemplating man in society, not merely the relations of the Spartans and Athenians between 431 and 404 B.C. Sallust was too deeply engrossed in the present, and, moreover, was a Roman; he could not abstract himself from the surroundings of which he was a part, nor, had he been able to, would his Roman nature have allowed him to make a universal history out of a Roman crisis. In consequence his works remain Roman histories and studies; and since he had not Thucydides' depth of insight, and centuries of moral philosophy had intervened, he fails to penetrate far below the surface; lust and ambition, which could be curbed if men but wanted, were held responsible for a crisis that was too complex and complicated for Sallust's understanding. The deterioration from the days of Cato he tries to explain by applying Thucydides' analysis of motives, and he does his best; a study of Thucydides' analysis of *stasis* would, if he had been able to stand aside from his present, have shown him how far he was from attaining to the penetration of his model. The influence of Cato and Thucydides on Sallust was the outcome of his present discontent, and his style the outcome of that influence; in happier times he would not have had to wrestle with the present; he could have taken a broader and more balanced view; had he not felt dissatisfaction with the present, he would not have had to turn to Cato and Thucydides to explain it, and he would have written in a different style.

Of Cicero we have already spoken, and there is little more to add. More than most other men he was imbued with the ideals of the Republic, the Republic of Scipio's day. In that atmosphere his spiritual and intellectual life is lived, to these standards he constantly refers the present when he passes judgement, and to this harmonious age he tries to restore his own discordant present. His style reflects the harmony and rhythm of those times; gracious and grand, musical yet manly, it represents the true *gravitas* of Rome at a time when that *gravitas* might seem to have passed from Roman life. While others were experimenting with different styles, Cicero produced a Latin style and vocabulary that reflected worthily Rome's greatness and her *gravitas*. As the disintegration became more complete, it was criticized, because it did not reflect the present; it was out of tune with the times. Bombastic and verbose it seemed;* too serene, they should have said, requiring leisure and education for its true appraisal.

For it was the urgent need to speak to the present in terms and ways that could be understood which I believe to have been the underlying reason for the development of the Attic style. Politics in these later years depended more than ever on the *plebs*; to them the politicians turned increasingly to get what the Senate would not grant; to the rowdy element men had recourse to force an issue which reason or prejudice had rejected; at no time could the *plebs* be easily ignored. Yet that part of the *plebs* which thronged the Comitia and comprised the audience of a *contio* was neither of sufficient education to appreciate or even understand well-rounded periods, nor had they the respect for the nobles which earlier had made them prepared to listen with half-comprehending ears to dignified addresses and to approve what they trustfully supposed to be the proper course. Mob oratory was now a need; a man must be able to harangue the *plebs* in its own terms and language, and to work upon its passions and its fears. The effect must be immediate; it was not a time to give measured arguments for men to brood upon before they gave their vote next day; their support and vote must be won at once or they would hoot and move away to other sport.*

Simplicity of style was thus essential; a speaker must speak with a directness that anyone could understand, so that none could be bewildered by complicated structure and nice subtleties. The Attic style was, I believe, the half-unconscious answer of the educated to this need. Rome, like Greece, was sensitive to style; if educated men must needs be simple in their style, then let the style be worthy of an educated man; thus from the needs of the moment sprang the Attic style at Rome, whose growing popularity in these last years Cicero himself attests.*

Cicero's place in politics we have discussed; we have noticed too his suggestion of the 'first' man endowed with such *auctoritas* that he could intervene to steady the ship of state without doing harm to the Republic's structure by arrogating to himself extra-constitutional power. That was in itself an admission that the State was far from well; for had the State been healthy, this would have happened of its own accord, as it had done in the past. It was owing to the sickness of the Republic that political power alone counted, that Pompeius without his army could be snubbed by the Senate, jeered at by Clodius and ignored unless he chose to join with those who held the power. *Auctoritas* and harmony go together; some man or men would have been exercising such influence if things had not been awry, and Cicero would not have had to suggest a solution which implied that things were well, and which could only have worked if they had been; he was prescribing not health but a symptom of health.

None the less his instinct was right; Augustus, for all his coldly calculating shrewdness, owed much of his success to his instinct for what chimed with Roman sentiment, and he not only pronounced in favour of Cicero's deep loyalty to the Republic,[1] he went further; for though we would agree with Syme[2] that Augustus did not seek his inspiration in political theory, and that his power and position were the consequence of careful calculation, not of generous sentiment, yet his sensitivity and shrewdness showed him what might and might not be, and he was at great pains to claim for himself as little as he could besides *auctoritas*. He knew that that was what Rome wanted, and he found the answer independently of Cicero; yet his emphasis on *auctoritas* confirmed Cicero's understanding.

But if in fact Augustus took much more than *auctoritas* to establish his position, that does not prove that Cicero was wrong or unaware of the needs of the time; it shows only that until the worst happens one hopes that a situation may be redeemed. Just as before the outbreak of a war men hope that it can be avoided, and sincere and able men pin their hopes to policies which the future shows to be of no avail, so until the final calamity Cicero and others like him hoped that the Republic could be restored to health and working order; Caesar knew better,[3] but had not the tact to conceal his knowledge, and therefore failed. Caesar was the consummation of the Populares' aims and methods; but his impatience would not wait nor stoop to subterfuge, and he succeeded in rousing what had long been dormant and had seemed quite dead, namely some feeling for the Republic and its ideals; not in many, but in some few, and the feeling grew in the next decades, warning Augustus not to imitate his great-uncle. Cicero could have helped Caesar, but Caesar had not time.

Cicero represented the old Republic, and his political works are

[1] Plut. *Cicero*, XLIX, 3–4: φιλόπατρις. [2] *Op. cit.* 318 ff.

[3] Cf. p. 150, n. 2 above and the sentence following: Sullam nescisse litteras qui dictaturam deposuerit.

a statement of its ideals, an encomium on its greatness. But it was the past, and in the form in which it was present in Cicero's mind it could not come back. Society cannot live on its past, though it may draw strength and inspiration from it; it must be forward-looking, with a faith and confidence in its future, based upon its past. Rome's destiny to Cicero was the past projected into the future, and therein lay no hope; to the Augustans, sick of civil war, looking with loving eyes at Rome's great past which had been marred by the malady now happily worked out, the future was full of hope and faith; Rome could continue with her interrupted mission; they must break with the immediate past and join themselves to their former greatness, expiating the sins of the last century. But Cicero was too early; he could not break with the present; all he could try to do was to join it to the past, and that was fatal; it could not be; it must be atoned for and forgotten in the happier past and greater future. The Augustans were luckier in this than Cicero, for Cicero must redeem the present, not condemn the past; they could pass judgement on the past and mark out Rome's future destiny in a world full of hope.

In Lucretius we see again the reflection of this age. We have pointed out how religion and society had parted company as Rome lost its attractive force, and men and women who felt the need of some belief turned to oriental religions; and those who, infected by the unhappy and uncertain times, themselves felt uncertainty and doubt about the future, turned to superstitious practices which claimed to read the future. Those who embarked upon a political career found the battle absorbed their whole activity; the desire to reach high office seemed to become their one ambition, involving them generally in debt and possibly in danger; a group of people living on their nerves in a restless city. We have seen also that many persons in disgust withdrew into the refuge of Epicureanism, which had been frowned upon in earlier years; Lucretius is their poet and apologist. He saw and felt the spirit of his times, the unhappiness which sought its consolation in strange religions and horoscopes, the discontent of those who had embarked upon a course whose end was not worth while, and the disgust of those who would not be active partners in such a life; and he trumpeted the message which could give happiness and peace to their restless and unhappy minds. With a fervour worthy of a missionary he set forth the philosophy of Epicurus, calling upon men to end their troubles by listening to the teaching of man's saviour. Yet, as I have pointed out, he was exhorting men to abandon their society, to leave others to maintain its structure, while they retired in selfish quietude, unruffled by the storms in which others were buffeted and perhaps wrecked. Such selfish, anti-social teaching could not become religion; it could only be what its creator intended, a refuge from a society that seemed to have neither attraction nor meaning. The poet who could write 'Suave mari magno, etc.'[1] at that moment has revealed himself, to whatever shifts of explanation he may resort. We need not blame him; the environment oppressed him and he must escape or die; it is escape he chooses, not society's salvation. In this age it seemed the only way to live an untroubled life; and merely to be free of strain and worry seemed so important then; he could not think of men's duties to society, for what could one man do in such surroundings? He must save himself, he could not save society.

That Epicureanism should find adherents and a poet now is proof sufficient of the sickness of the times; in better times it could not win a Roman's allegiance; it was a counsel of despair, suited to the times but not to Rome. Horace and Virgil had found themselves in their earlier days in sympathy with Epicureanism; but when the times became peaceable and the air was filled once more with faith and hope, they turned to Stoicism, the Roman's proper philosophy.* In this too the Augustan Age turned its back on this unhappy generation; as Caesar's form of government, as Catullus' poems were rejected as non-Roman,* so was Epicureanism turned out of doors for being anti-social. Lucretius suffered their fate; they hardly mentioned him; all three were true to their generation; but the Augustan Age was true to Rome.

[1] II, 1 ff.

CONCLUSION

Thus concludes our study of the Republic's failure, a failure of the spirit, not of government, if we have understood it aright, which found its end and solution only when the Age of Augustus gave back to men the opportunity—for the wish had long been there—to live once again in conformity with their former moral code, to take up again the ideas and ideals of their happier past and give them life and purpose in an even greater future.

The Republic's crisis and failure have an interest for others than the specialist; for they were a crisis and a failure of society, and hence their interest extends to all societies and all students of society in every age. A society is more than the individuals that compose it, though it has no existence independently of them. 'What is a city without men?' asked Sophocles;[1] it is equally pertinent to ask what are men without a city, i.e. a society; for only in a society does man find the opportunity to live a full life, to give full expression to all his talents, be they great or small, and to realize the best that is in him by living not merely among, but for, others. In a society he is able to give a loyalty and devotion to certain ideals which embody his faith and aspirations; and it is the sharing of those ideals by all its members which gives life to the society. Societies take long to come to being; it is not at once that the material circumstances of men's lives mould and are moulded until they and the men who live with and by them come to know each other and be welded into one; and in this process the ideals of the people are slowly fashioned, until at last there emerges a society with its own values, its own aspirations and its own faith.

But society is a sensitive organism; remove or destroy the unifying element, and it breaks into a thousand pieces; men still live together, but the cement which bound them into one is gone.

[1] *Oed. Tyr.* 56–7 (paraphrased).

And there is much in man that is selfish and disruptive; he lives largely by his instincts and emotions, and when the highest of these instincts loses its object, he is left only with those more animal ones by which to live. Live he does, at a lower level, harnessing his powers to attain his baser ends, conspiring and combining with some the better to accomplish his purpose against others. This happens in any society when its ideals are shattered, as it did in Rome; but once the faith is shaken and destroyed, it cannot be replaced to order; it can only be won again by suffering and experience. For a time things can seem to be well, until the last of the spiritual capital is spent; but when the final cheque has been drawn, society is bankrupt, and the consequences must ensue; before the society can come together once again, fresh capital must be created.

This was what happened at Rome as a result of what the Gracchi did. Tiberius' challenge to the Senate, made in the way in which it was, involved a challenge to the harmony of Rome's society, of which the Senate was so important a part; for inevitably the question must arise whether the Senate should be governing the Roman world; and the mob is not the best arbiter on so grave a matter. Yet to the mob Tiberius went, supposing that nothing but his legislation was at stake; his shrewder brother, and hence more culpable, of deliberate intent set his face against the Senate, and thought it clever to have raised the Equites against that body; what his shrewdness did not tell him—or so at least, in his defence, we hope—was that he had provoked a question which must now be solved before all others; and the answer to that question took a hundred years to find. The clash of groups came into being, and nothing could heal the wound the body politic had sustained; the contest for the power at Rome made it impossible for Rome to be in harmony, and the longer it continued, the worse became the disintegration, the lower the depths to which persons were prepared to go in their own or their group's interest. The ideals which had made of Rome a society evaporated into near-nothingness, and Rome was a society only in name. What is surprising is the essential vitality of the Roman spirit, which after more than fifty years of strife and civil war emerged again as tough and strong as ever, like an acorn from beneath a concrete slab, to create the Augustan Age and make possible the Roman Empire.

Yet Rome could not sever herself from her past; what had been had been; the present was the child of the past, and Cicero's Republic could never more come into being. Facts and sentiments were to be constantly at war; with Augustus as the personal saviour of society they might seem to have agreed like lamb and wolf to live together; but the deep opposition between the two could not be obscured or denied for ever; as time passed, the antagonism became ever more open until in Tacitus we see the fatalistic acquiescence in the facts against which the spirit revolted —in vain. This was the final consequence of what the Gracchi did —the death of the Republic. No society can break with its past and start again; if it changes—and change there must assuredly be —it must remain the same thing. England was more fortunate than Rome; in its greatest crises and convulsions its leading men knew this instinctively, and the more violent the break with the past, the more anxious were they to unite themselves with that past by spiritual bonds.[1]

The Romans, too, had that instinct; the Gracchi unfortunately did not; once the disaster had begun, it had to run its course; and when the Roman spirit had its chance to show itself once more, it did its best, but the body was maimed. It is a measure of the gravity of what the Gracchi did that the Roman spirit was unable to react in time; if Scipio's humanism was provoked to bless Tiberius' murder and call down a curse on any that should imitate him, we may be sure that what Tiberius had done seemed a far more terrible thing than many historians suppose. But Scipio's curse proved only to be part of the greater Gracchan curse; Caius died as Scipio's curse required; but bloodshed and strife only multiplied themselves to bring destruction on the Republic Scipio's curse was invoked to save; and once begun there

[1] See Butterfield, *The Englishman and his History*.

was no staying it. The Roman spirit, conservative, instinctive, emerged from the carnage of the civil wars to regain itself, and though it could not exorcise the past, it tried to link itself to the further past to create a better future; no new written constitution, no theory to justify or limit Augustus' power, but a feeling with the sensitive antennae of the spirit after what was best and Roman; and their efforts, though only in part did they succeed, gave us the Roman Empire and our Western civilization.

NOTES

NOTES

3]

'*quis iustius induit arma*'. Lucan I, 126–7, speaking of the responsibility for the Civil War between Caesar and Pompeius.

5]

its unmourned end. I say 'unmourned' because, as I shall show below, the ideal of the Republic continued to live in the minds only of a few; for the rest it became mainly a catchword to conceal the facts of partisan strife. The great majority were well satisfied with Augustus' idea of *res publica restituta* and sought nothing but the emotion excited by the word *res publica*. The imperial worshippers of the Republic mourned not the true loss but an imagined loss which contained all that they missed in their day.

7]

cast their votes in a particular way. Hence the laws against electoral bribery, beginning with the Lex Cornelia Baebia of 181 B.C.

9]

it was not general. See, for instance, Polybius, VI, 56, where he admits that most Romans believe in their gods; he tries to explain away the nobles' attitude in a way typical of a Greek rationalist, by suggesting that it is to keep the people in check. But he really disproves his own explanation by pointing out that the scrupulous honesty of Roman magistrates was due to their deep respect for their oath.

without that outside help. This feeling is again very strong in Virgil, who has this sense of Rome's destiny strongly marked; and the Augustan Age was an integrated society.

10]

known to us from Ennius. Cf. such lines in Ennius as: qualis consiliis quantumque potesset in armis (Vahlens[3], 222; Warmington, *Remains of Old Latin* I, Loeb, 271); quem nemo ferro potuit superare nec auro (Vahlens, 373; Warmington, 209); fortes Romani sunt tamquam caelus profundus (Vahlens, 546; Warmington, 470); moribus antiquis stat res Romana virisque (Vahlens 500; Warmington, 467). Greatness in counsel and war, courage and incorruptibility, unflinching bravery, all based on the traditional upbringing and way of life and also on the quality of its men. Ennius is most important as both giving expression to the ideal and by that fact also laying down the pattern for others to follow. Kipling in a different way did something similar for Englishmen.

14]

an individual writer. Cf. Bignone, *St. della Lett. Lat.* II, 78–9. By 'individual' writer I mean one who writes about himself and expresses personal views and criticisms, etc. Ennius had shown originality but, so far as we can infer, was rather introducing Romans to new views and ideas, culled from Greece, than himself expressing views (though he may have agreed with the views he did express) in an atmosphere of conflicting ideas; he was educating Romans rather than asserting his own views.

18]

to a foreign world. I have omitted to mention oratory here, since its publication was incidental, and then, too, for political purposes, to put on record one's own policy and the shortcomings of one's political opponents.

22]

not have held so firmly together. One may compare the beliefs of the different classes in England in the second half of the nineteenth century. It was a Christian society, yet the degrees of belief were many, and among many of the educated persons there was much rationalizing. There were some, both clergy and lay, who were aware that *expedit esse deos, et ut expedit esse putemus*, since it helped to keep the people in control. But most Victorians were Christians, and were aware that the harmony of their society depended on this common religion which gave meaning and purpose to the society. To psycho-analyse the Victorians and pronounce them hypocrites would show only our own religious failure and our inability to understand their society.

put to political use. The Lex Aelia Fufia, which seems to have allowed 'obnuntiatio' to prevent legislation, shows how closely intertwined politics and religion were, and how religious obstructions could be used to thwart what was felt to be pernicious legislation; it should not, however, be assumed that it was the result of calculating cynicism rather than a sincere belief that Heaven should and would prevent destructive tendencies in the State. But it could, and did, lead, later on, to a purely cynical use of 'obnuntiatio' by politicians.

23]

admiration of Polybius. See above, note to p. 9. Q. Mucius Scaevola, following Panaetius (see Pohlenz, *Die Stoa*, 198, 262), remarked that there were three classes of gods, that of the poets, of the philosophers, and of the statesmen (Augustine, *De Civ. Dei*, IV, 27). This is later, but even so, we need to be careful of over-great cynicism; it was a simple statement of fact, not stating disbelief on the part of any group. As I have pointed out, the degrees of belief were many, and the statesmen had to respect the form of belief of the uneducated.

33]

divine machinery. In fact, Rome had not reached the stage of sophistication when divine machinery could be regarded as conventional; such an idea presupposes a considerable literary maturity and a considerable literature, both of which were absent from Rome.

48]

so they might from the East. Macedon's alliance with Carthage during the late war only made this more obvious to her. The bitterness and the critical nature of the Hannibalic War naturally made Rome at this moment particularly sensitive to threats to her security, and that was why she fought Philip. When Holleaux, *C.A.H.* VIII, 239, says that had Rome been more keen-sighted and less easily alarmed, she would not have come to dominate the Hellenistic world, but would more probably have concentrated her efforts in the neighbouring barbarian countries of the West, he raises an interesting thesis for a *controversia*, but it ignores the mainspring of Rome's actions at this time. She turned East because she was apprehensive of danger from there, not because she wanted to create an empire. Had she not felt fear, she would not have moved. And since no desire for expansion moved her, she would not have done anything more in the West than she did in fact do. She dealt with the tribes on her northern frontier and in Spain because it was necessary to do so for her security and that of her province. More than that she would not have done in any case; had she been able to sit quietly within Italy, she would have done; there was as yet no imperial policy.

whatever system of leagues and alliances she pleased. Though Rome progressively narrowed the limits of the 'free' area not only in Greece but elsewhere, as she came slowly to discover that control of one sphere generally requires control of many spheres. See Sherwin White, *The Roman Citizenship*, 149–63, where he shows how Rome came to impose limitations on the concept of *libertas* in relation to *civitates liberae.*

49]

proves both her moderation. One may contrast Rome's behaviour with that of Greece and the Hellenistic kingdoms during their age of power; with them conquest and the extension of their territories were the mainsprings of their action; this is true of the Athenian, Spartan and Theban hegemonies, and of the wars between the different Hellenistic monarchs; power and aggrandizement were the aim and object. The conflict between Rome and these monarchies represented a conflict that went deeper than the surface appearance, and it was not for some time that the Hellenistic world came to realize this; Rome never did. See below, note to p. 56.

51]

which none can now prevent. As was the case with the Hellenistic kingdoms; the check on them was the existence of the others, which led to an unstable equilibrium based on a balance of power.

as happened in Rome and the U.S.A. The point of difference which I wish particularly to emphasize is the moral one, the acceptance of responsibility for others, which is not to be found in powerful States, and represents a tremendous moral and spiritual advance.

a century's civil discord. The change from the outlook of a powerful State to that of a world-power can be admirably seen in the case of the U.S.A. Sir Winston Churchill once pointed out that the U.S.A., with a tithe of her post-war expenditure, could, had she chosen, have made the Second World War impossible. But the U.S.A. was then merely a powerful State; she had entered the First World War in self-defence, had withdrawn into isolation after 1922, feeling no responsibility for what happened in Europe, provided her own safety was not directly involved, and was at first prepared to stand aside in the second war, until she was herself attacked. But on the morrow of the end of that war she assumed all the responsibilities of the Western world; she became, in fact, consciously a world-power, which she could have been in 1920, but for which she was mentally and morally not yet adjusted.

52]

a terrible thing. See *Sibylline Oracles*, IV, 105–6:

καὶ σύ, τάλαινα Κόρινθε, τεήν ποτ' ἐπόψει ἅλωσιν,
Καρχηδών, καὶ σεῖο χαμαὶ γόνυ πύργος ἐρείσει.

Polybius, XXXVI, 9 (referring to the destruction of Carthage, but that of Corinth must have been equally in men's minds); Sherwin White, *op. cit.* 234.

the days of their greatness. One must remember that the destruction of the city = destruction of the State. This is not possible with us, and we therefore have to solve the problem of the treatment of the vanquished differently.

53]

supported Massinissa against Carthage. It is to be admitted that in 152 B.C. they had compelled Massinissa to restore to Carthage territory taken from her; but by then the question was becoming more urgent, and the opposing policies (referred to below in the text) were crystallizing.

threaten her security. The theory that Rome destroyed Carthage to prevent it falling into the hands of Massinissa has little to commend it. If Rome had been so fearful of Massinissa, she would have dealt directly with him; it is assuming a subtlety in foreign policy which Rome did not show at this time; she preserved a balance of power where she thought her interests required it, but she dealt directly with what she thought represented a danger to herself. Nor had she any need to employ such indirect methods to deal with a small king such as Massinissa; the truth is that she encouraged Massinissa as a counterpoise to the supposed threat of Carthage.

56]

not increase Rome's income. Admittedly Romans and Italians in course of time congregated in considerable numbers to pursue their business; but it is very certain that the Senate did not have this prospect in mind when it declared Delos a free port.

aimed at hurting no one. A further factor which was now becoming apparent to the Greek world was the wholly different attitude of Rome from that of the Greeks towards war and its object. What I may call the rules of war were clearly understood and accepted in the Hellenistic world; if one felt strong enough, one attacked one's neighbour, and hoped to seize part of his territories to swell one's own; at a certain point one side would realize that it was in a losing posture, and a peace would be agreed upon, until the next war broke out. Both diplomacy and war followed accepted rules and conventions. But Rome was an 'outsider' in this as in so much else; she went to war because she was apprehensive of a possible threat, and would not stop until she had got rid of the source of her apprehension; there was no breaking off in the middle, as Antiochus discovered; and the corollary was that Rome pursued war to the point of destruction, if necessary, of her opponent. The dawning consciousness of this fact moved Rhodes to her stand in the war against Perseus.

62]

it preferred slaves. Just as at the beginning of the Industrial Revolution machines ousted workmen from their jobs.

64]

a philosopher than a statesman. As I have pointed out, it was as a moral problem, susceptible of a solution based on philosophical theory, that it presented itself. It was not seen as primarily an economic problem.

otherwise have been left to starve. We may profitably quote an extract from Greville's diary to illustrate the difficulty of dealing with economic problems which have social consequences, even in an age which was aware of economic factors. Greville was Secretary of the Privy Council, and more concerned than many with social problems. Under 17 February 1832, we read this: 'A man came yesterday from Bethnal Green with an account of that district. They are all weavers, forming a sort of separate community.... They neither emigrate nor change their occupation; they can do nothing else.... They are for the most part out of employment, and can get none.... The parish is in debt; every day adds to the number of paupers and diminishes that of rate-payers.... The district is in a complete state of insolvency and hopeless poverty.... *Government is ready to interpose with assistance, but what can Government do? We asked the man who came what could be done for them. He said "employment", and employment is impossible'* (the italics are mine). We should not be too hasty in criticizing the Roman nobles for making life possible for the dispossessed, even if they failed to prevent further dispossession.

65]

actively despised. Even though it may be unofficially indulged in through intermediaries, as it was by some Senators at least. We may compare the behaviour of the countess in *The Way of all Flesh*; having sold her Consols, she secretly invested in railway shares, increased the capital, and then reinvested in the sort of investment which the code of the time permitted to persons of her station.

67]

a way that none could censure. One may think of the action taken by Parliament after the disclosures which came to light in the impeachment of Warren Hastings.

68]

for Roman citizenship. The growing interference of the Roman government in such matters as could not otherwise be properly controlled was probably not felt very keenly, since the formalities were preserved and action taken through the local authorities. It was in fact making Rome the central government of a municipal system; but it occurred to neither side to change the relationship, since the development was slow; and the solution of universal Roman citizenship was almost revolutionary to the mentality of city-states. But in view of their close co-operation with Rome they wanted a more favourable treaty.

71]

passages in the later books. XVIII, 35, 1 ff.; XXXI, 25, 3 ff. It is not known when these books were written or published, but, if *c.* 155 B.C. is assumed as the date for the publication of Bks. I–VI, it seems likely that these later books were written not earlier than the 140's B.C. By then the effects of the Carthaginian War and its aftermath would be beginning to be felt. See Walbank and Brink's article in *C.Q.*, XLVIII, 1954, 97 ff.

with temporary emergency powers. It is important to appreciate this Roman method of solving novel problems; they were always most reluctant to introduce novelties, and far preferred to give a fresh meaning to what existed; hence the use made in this century of the legal fiction.

72]

was posed by the Gracchi. It is most instructive to compare the history of England between 1820 and 1850. One discovers there all the failings, weakness, corruption, etc., that we find at Rome at this moment. Electoral bribery and corruption (at first even greater after the Reform Bill of 1832), social and political influence in Church appointments and a worldliness in the Church, a considerable group of the governing class, the Tories, bitterly hostile to the slightest change, an economic revolution with serious social consequences, an irresponsible attitude owing to the defeat of Napoleon, the greatest wealth in the world combined with the greatest poverty (a fact noted by contemporaries), a multitude of phenomena, in fact, which suggested that a new epoch was coming painfully to birth. Yet because in England reform came slowly after bitter fights, with the defeated side accepting defeat, those years of dangerous instability were the precursors of England's greatest period in history; whereas Rome slid into civil war and revolution and her whole course of history was changed. Only a very stubborn defender of the Gracchi would maintain that there were not peradventure ten Whigs at Rome; with patience, and pressure from the liberal Senators, Rome could have emerged as did England: *Gracchis aliter visum.*

75]

power and personal advantage. The moral, spiritual and political crisis of the opening of this period has a close and instructive analogy in the England of the 1830's. In both cases there was a relaxation of tension as a result of the removal of an outside threat and the resulting feeling that they could take things more easily; in both cases there were serious political and social consequences of an economic revolution, whose motion they could not control and whose worst effects they knew not how to lessen. The struggle for the Reform Bill is very similar to the struggle for land distribution, because in both cases it was mistakenly supposed that the measure would alleviate the distress of the revolution. The struggle and the fierce opposition of the Tories to the Reform Bill is well known; but eventually they had the wisdom to give way, because they knew that they really had no choice. Laelius' attempt to pass a land law may be compared to Lord John Russell's first abortive attempt at reform. But suppose that there had been some dormant and antiquated means of legislating independently of the Houses by means of the London mob, and to this means Russell had had recourse. The result would have been immediate; both Whigs and Tories would have combined against Russell and his mob of London supporters, since both parties would have realized the threat to themselves. The history of England from that moment would have been very similar to that of Rome after 133 B.C. Contemporary writings show the bewilderment in England at this time of those who were sincerely concerned at conditions and were apprehensive of discontent breaking out into revolution; they would gladly have done something, had they known what; but they knew not what to do.

77]

what it set out to do. It was, as I have pointed out above, a philosopher's answer, and would not have solved the problem; but time alone would show them that. It would have had an excellent psychological effect, just as did the first Reform Bill, even though it did not solve the problems many of its supporters hoped of it. The Gracchan legislation failed to achieve this end for reasons which we shall discuss below.

English aristocracy in the 1830's. It is interesting to quote Crispin's note in his Delphin edition, 1833, on Macer's speech, sec. 18, in Sallust's fragments: Utinam vero hodie Macer aliquis exoriretur, qui inerti et impudenti nobilitati non istud modo ingereret, sed eo vanissimos homines, de quibus tantum verba facio, ad parentum virtutes compelleret.

78]

Rome's new position. I take the proclamation as an example; the fact that there were divergent opinions in Rome on the policy which should be pursued, which caused political conflict during these years, serves only to emphasize the point that she felt compelled to go further than mere considerations of self-defence required in order to assure her security.

79]

fair and just to her subjects. The institution of this *quaestio* is sometimes quoted as an indication of moral deterioration in the governors of provinces. But there were cases of bad behaviour before this time; it represented rather a determination to keep a tighter control of governors than hitherto. Similarly the institution of the National Society for the Prevention of Cruelty to Children indicated, not an increasing cruelty to children, but an increasing concern to prevent what cruelty there was, which had been condoned in the past.

82]

precedent and usage. The Senate's direct constitutional power was very slight, though its indirect power, based upon its predominance over many years, was immense. But any challenge to the first must inevitably lead to a considerable weakening of the second in course of time.

yet his laws were passed. His deposition of Octavius was the final challenge to any authority but his own; the tribunician veto had been one of the methods by which the Senate had contrived to retain control in spite of the possible threat of independent legislation; when that was successfully challenged, the Senate could do nothing. It was one man against the accumulated wisdom of the Senate; and the chances were that the accumulated wisdom would be more salutary than the one man.

considerations of foreign policy. And handled it, if we may accept Plut. *Tib. Gracchus*, XIV, 2, in a very impudent way, calculated to emphasize the Senate's lack of powers in the matter.

83]

should have continued dormant. The action of the tribunes in 157 B.C. (App. *Iber.* 49; Livy, *Per.* 48) and 138 B.C. (Livy, *Per.* 55; *Epit. Ox.* 204) in imprisoning the consuls because of the army levy does not in any way provide a precedent for Tib. Gracchus' behaviour. These tribunes were really exercising their primary function of protecting the people; since there was felt to be considerable hardship and discontent, they acted in a constitutional and proper way, and thus drew attention to the inadequacy of the present system. They made no attempt to dictate by independent legislation how the army was to be recruited; they left that to the Senate.

85]

men who had done no wrong. Tiberius Gracchus has another importance for the student of Roman history, an importance which may be mentioned here because it also partially explains the opposition to his measures which he provoked. He was the only Roman to put his faith in theory and to attempt to apply to a problem the remedy which theoretical idealism suggested. His close connexion with Blossius and Stoic ideas led him to suppose that what seemed good on paper was necessarily best and right for Rome in practice; and like other idealists who do not understand the workings of their society he found himself driven to extremes in order to overcome what seemed to him to be narrow, partisan opposition. The belief that theoretical constitutions and plans could be successfully imposed on society was, like the origins of this particular plan, Greek, and basically opposed to the Roman character; the plan provoked an opposition on the part of many Romans, whose instinct told them that this was not good for the body politic.

It is neither sufficient nor accurate to speak of those who opposed him as being selfish and 'reactionary'; some were; but others had begun by supporting him; Scipio's attitude was one of hostility; yet he was among the most progressive men of his generation—but a progressive *Roman*. The Roman political instinct felt its way towards that solution of its problems which was conformable to the spirit and *ethos* of its society; the settlement of Augustus is perhaps the clearest example of this. This instinctive feeling cannot give its justification in terms of reason, though by reason the Romans not infrequently sought to 'rationalize' what they had done; Scipio and those who opposed Gracchus because they could feel the un-Romanness of his ideas and means, could not justify their opposition by arguments drawn from reason; and when judgement is passed on the Gracchan episode, reason, marshalling her arguments on both sides, tends to pronounce judgement in favour of the 'would-be-reformer' against the 'selfish reactionaries'. Thus this first attempt to apply the precepts of reason and thus work against the Roman grain was, through the opposition it provoked, responsible for setting in train the movement which led to the downfall of the Republic.

This is not to say that some solution not unsimilar in its aim and achievement could not have come to pass at Rome; Laelius had himself proposed something similar, and it is a great pity that Fate has not vouchsafed us any details of his plan; the answer, had not Tiberius forced the issue, would almost certainly have come and been a Roman answer, doing no violence to the Roman spirit, just as the Reform Bill in England was the English answer to the problem it set out to solve, and not a doctrinaire scheme based on ideas of Athenian democracy or of the French Revolution. Grote saw Athenian democracy through the eyes of an English Liberal; Gracchus chose Blossius rather than Panaetius, to whom Laelius and the Scipionic circles owed so much.

87]

their own ends. E.g. the use of the words 'res publica', 'libertas', 'factio', etc., by all parties in the last decades of the Republic. Similarly Communists talk of democracy, workers' rights, freedom, etc., deluding those who are convinced that these are good, but who do not understand their essence; it thus becomes possible to destroy democracy in the name of democracy.

88]

self than group. Cf. Caelius' significant remark, *Ad Fam.* VIII, 14, 3: Illud te non arbitror fugere quin homines in dissensione domestica debeant, quam diu civiliter sine armis certetur, honestiorem sequi partem, ubi ad bellum et castra ventum sit, firmiorem et id melius statuere quod tutius sit.

89]

fame and a triumph. Cf. Cicero's description of Macedonia, *In Pis.* XIX, 44, as a province 'quae fuerit ex omnibus una maxime triumphalis'.

hatred of Rome in their hearts. There are repeated references both in Cicero and the historians to the hatred felt towards Rome by the outside world during these years; cf. also the Sibylline Oracles, some of which date from this period.

90]

provincials whom they despised. Cf. the complaints and miseries of the Allobroges, '*publice privatimque* aere alieno oppressos' (Sallust, *Cat.* XL, 1 ff.); they were prepared to do anything, 'dum ea res civitatem aere alieno liberaret' (sec. 4).

the provincial governors. Their monopoly lasted until Sulla restored the courts to the Senate, whose behaviour was by now no better; Pompeius divided the juries between the Senate, the Equites and the *tribuni aerarii*; but heavy bribery was now indulged in, and the financial power of the Equites was very great indeed.

most other Romans would have done. Brutus and Cassius, the great Republicans, were as adept as anyone at wringing money from their provinces.

as selfish as their squabbles. It is during this period that the Roman attitude to Greeks and other foreigners became one of contempt; they were treated as lesser breeds, fit only to be slaves or conquered subjects of Rome. Cf. Cicero, *In Verrem*, II, 2, 7; *Pro Flacco*, VIII, 18 f., 27 f., 66; *Pro Fonteio*, XV, 33; *Pro Scauro*, throughout; and elsewhere. This attitude helps to explain the prevalent behaviour of nearly all Romans in the provinces and abroad.

unhappy and powerless. Cf. for instance, Cicero, *Pro Flacco*, XII, 27; Flaccus had been accused of demanding money as a contribution to the fleet: 'Utrum igitur hoc Graeci statuent aut aliae exterae nationes, an nostri praetores, nostri duces, nostri imperatores?' It seems to have been axiomatic that the provincials should have no say in their own government.

93]

which the city provided. Cf. Sallust, *Cat.* XXXVII, 7: praeterea iuventus, quae in agris manuum mercede inopiam toleraverat, privatis atque publicis largitionibus excita, urbanum otium ingrato labori praetulerat.

94]

with which Cicero has made us so familiar. We are speaking here of that considerable part of the *plebs urbana* whose hooligan behaviour is so well known to us from the sources. But there must have been many people, shopkeepers, labourers, etc., who led quiet lives, doing their work and taking little part in the political activities of the time. They were in Rome rather than of it; and while from one point of view their existence is important, from our point of view they were without effect or influence either for good or ill on Rome.

96]

Rome and Britain have both realized. The view taken in the following brief review of the war is based on De Sanctis, 'Sallustio e la Guerra di Giugurtha', in *Problemi di Storia Antica*, 187–214.

97]

to limit the war. Sallust, *Jug.* XL, 1: ...ut quaereretur in eos quorum consilio Jugurtha senati decreta neglegisset, quique ab eo in legationibus aut imperiis pecunias accepissent; qui elephantos quique profugas tradidissent; item qui de pace aut bello cum hostibus pactiones fecissent.

opponents of the war. We cannot be certain as to the composition of the jury in this inquiry; but I have followed De Sanctis, *op. cit.* 202.

98]

useful political purposes. The Lex Domitia de sacerdotiis of 104 B.C. It was part of the disaster of this political struggle that everything was dragged down to the political level. Religion, instead of standing apart from party considerations, was pulled into the squalor of party politics, to the great hurt both of itself and of society.

'*maiestas populi Romani*'. The Lex Appuleia de maiestate of 103 B.C. (?). While nothing could excuse the behaviour of Mallius and Caepio, yet the other disasters were due partly to the inability of amateur generals to contend with serious military situations, and to the fact that the Senate, thanks to the Equites, was involved in a very difficult war at the same time in Numidia. Marius was fortunate in having two years in which to give his undivided attention to preparations for the struggle; there is no reason to doubt that Metellus would have been as successful as was Marius, had the Senate been free to choose him for the war against the Germans.

99]

distinction for the holder. The consulship also, of course, represented the greatest *imperium*, and gave the holder all the rights and responsibilities of the chief Republican office.

100]

the professional army. For the general question of the army at the time of Marius' reform, see Gabba, *Athenaeum*, n.s. XXVII (1949), 173–209; and for the post-Marian army, Gabba, *Athenaeum*, n.s. XXIX (1951), 171–272.

101]

best form of pension. I believe that Saturninus had little more in mind than the winning of political support, and that he thought of land allotment because it had proved popular with the Gracchi.

unknown at Rome. Scipio Africanus Maior's troops who had fought *overseas* for long periods had been recompensed; Livy, XXXI, 4, 1–3; 49, 5–6; XXXII, 1, 6. This was really a form of rehabilitation for genuine farmers who had been away from their farms for many years. Soldiers had also been settled in Spain during the second century, at Gracchuris (Livy, *Epit.* 41; Fest. p. 86, 52); at Carteia (Livy, XLIII, 3); at Corduba (Strabo, III, 2, 1); at Palma and Pollentia in the Balearic Isles (Strabo, III, 5, 1). To the extent to which this shows a developing policy on the part of the Senate, it makes Saturninus' behaviour all the more irresponsible, converting policy into election politics. The Senate had used retired soldiers to help by colonization in the settlement of Spain, and this policy could have continued in a normal fashion both in Spain and in other parts of the West.

should apply to army veterans. Last, *C.A.H.* IX, 136 says that 'if it is their (i.e. soldiers') good fortune to survive till the age when they are too old for further active service, they may reasonably expect some provision to be made for their declining years'. It is, perhaps, unfair to argue in terms of what seems reasonable to us in this issue. Other citizens did not have 'provision made for their declining years'; they either saved, went on working, were supported by relatives and their *patronus*, or survived by a combination of these means. There was little 'reasonable' to contemporaries about the suggestion; it must somehow justify itself. Saturninus probably made the original suggestion in 103 B.C. to win support for himself and Marius (if Gabba, *op. cit.* 205 is right that the large enrolments for Marius' army occurred in 103 B.C., this would almost certainly be his motive), and without originality used the Gracchan idea of a land allotment.

102]

many certainly would not be. Last, *loc. cit.* 137, says: 'Sulla sought it (i.e. the solution of the problem of the veterans) in vain, and it was left for the genius of Augustus, by instituting the *aerarium militare*, to make the state itself responsible for pensions in a way which rendered it unnecessary for the troops to pin their hopes on any individual.' This is, perhaps, an unfair criticism, for it ignores the wholly different circumstances of the two periods. The spiritual atmosphere of Augustan Rome was that of an integrated society, in which political quarrels between classes and individuals had disappeared. Since Augustus had made himself supreme head of the army, he was merely organizing in the best way possible, without fear of rivalry, a responsibility which the Republican generals had had to face in a different way. It was common sense and practical efficiency rather than genius. If Sulla had instituted an *aerarium militare*, it would have succeeded no better than any of his other constitutional reforms; competing generals would still have won their soldiers' loyalty by bribes and promises. Nothing could have succeeded; the fault was in the age. Had there been a competitor to Augustus, the *aerarium militare* would not have helped him, as was seen when rival contestants arose for the Imperial purple.

104]

a problem of statesmanship. The neglect of the Italian problem was one of the most unfortunate consequences of the disintegration. It was now so wrapped round with political implications that the Senate had done nothing. Tib. Gracchus had put an end to the good relations between the governing classes of Rome and the Italian cities; and though Scipio had stepped in, relations were never really restored. C. Gracchus seems to have tried to meet the Italians' wishes, but his methods had reduced it to a narrow political level, and it continued so. The nobles were not prepared to deal with it, because of the possible effect upon the Comitia of so many additional voters, and these were the terms in which they now thought. It is possible that but for the Gracchi and their continuators there might have been no Italian problem; that relations could have been amicably modified, as they had been down to 133 B.C. But it is certainly true that as things were no group at Rome had, so far as is known, given a thought to the Italians for thirty years; they were all far too concerned with their political squabbles.

105]

marched his professional army. It is certainly not true that this army followed Sulla because it depended upon him for its grant of land; it followed him because it feared that Marius might take other soldiers on what it was hoped would be a lucrative campaign.

107]

the irresponsibility of tribunician legislation. Whether tribunes completely lost the right of submitting bills to the people, or were restricted by having to gain Senatorial approval for their bill need not concern us here; it was probably the latter, but that was enough to attain Sulla's purpose.

109]

ensured efficiency in the present. Down to the end of the second Punic War emergencies of this kind had been met by the appointment of a Dictator. In the second century a similar end had been attained by organizing the appointment of the right man to the consulship, e.g. Scipio Aemilianus in 135 B.C. But since the intrusion of the Populares into political life, this method had necessarily lost most of its attraction and utility. Popular insistence had helped the Senate in its appointment of Scipio; the Senate could do with its own safeguards what no one else in Rome had power to do. But by the time of Marius the people had an alternative and opposed means of getting their nominee appointed, and thus there were two rival systems. Sulla had given back to the Senate its control, but since in its own interests he had laid down strict conditions for the holding of the consulship, the Senate could not hope that the right man would always be eligible for the consulship at the right moment.

110]

or the consulship. He was sent 'pro consule' (Cic. *De Pomp. Imp.* 62). But at this time all pro-magistrates were 'pro consule'; see Willems, *Le Sénat de la République romaine*, II, 571, n. 5.

112]

without a leader. Sall. *Cat.* XXXIX, 1 f.: 'Sed postquam Cn. Pompeius ad bellum maritumum atque Mithridaticum missus est, plebis opes imminutae, paucorum potentia crevit. Ei magistratus, provincias aliaque omnia tenere, ipsi innoxii, florentes, sine metu aetatem agere ceterosque iudiciis terrere, quo plebem in magistratu placidius tractarent.' This passage shows the importance to the Populares of having a leader, one who would be the focal point for their activities, and shows also how the nobles, fearful of Pompeius, consolidated their position during his absence, and thus ushered in the final decade of the fatal struggle for power.

close-knit opposition to contend with. The importance of Pompeius to the cause of the Populares was shown in the failure of the attempt by Crassus and Caesar to create a counterpoise to Pompeius' strength by the Rullan bill. It was sufficient for Cicero to show the people the threat to their darling for it to be rejected. The success of the nobles in consolidating their position was seen in the well organized and successful opposition to Pompeius, against which even a tribune trying to legislate on his behalf in 60 B.C. was powerless.

expedite both these requests. In the major wars of the second century the Senate had sent out ten commissioners who, in consultation with the general, had drawn up the terms of peace and arranged for the administration of the new province. During the Spanish War Roman generals had on occasions made arrangements without reference to the Senate, though the Senate had to ratify any such agreement, and their refusal to do so meant that the agreement had no validity, as e.g. Mancinus' agreement in 137 B.C. This practice had continued during the Jugurthine War, and generals who had made agreements with the enemy without the sanction of the Senate were involved in the Mamilian inquiry; and the Senate made it clear that any such agreements were not valid without the consent of the Senate and people (Sall. *Jug.* XXXIX, 3). By the first century, however, the practice seems to have been dropped; there is only one authenticated case, that of Lucullus, to whom ten commissioners were sent to organize Eastern affairs; and we may here suspect political pressure. Lucullus was by this time the object of attack at Rome in consequence largely of the Equites' hostility; his opponents may have insisted on taking away from him his independence in this matter. This would explain, perhaps, what Cicero (*Ad. Att.* XIII, 6 A) noted as strange in the composition of this commission, namely that it contained relatives of Lucullus; the Senate may have been forced to appoint the commission, but have done their best on Lucullus' behalf. But in view of the normal practice at this time, there was no excuse for holding up the ratification of Pompeius' *acta*.

113]

the first triumvirate. The nobles showed the precise limits of their policy in 60 B.C. They thought that in the last five years they had sufficiently consolidated their position to be able to beat their enemies, and they now took up arms against the Populares and the Equestrian Order. But for Caesar they might have succeeded. Yet it made clear that there was now no hope of agreement through good will or prudent compromise.

115]

redraft the constitution. He had been named 'Dictator legibus scribundis et rei publicae constituendae'. But Pompeius would have had to be named Dictator for some purpose, and it would have been difficult to name any purpose under the circumstances which could exclude political reform; Sulla's precedent therefore would have been a strong allurement.

116]

the Republic as its watchword. There is a certain symbolic significance in the fact that Caesar was claiming, *inter alia*, to be protecting the tribune's rights, while Pompeius was the champion of the Senate; in other words, the two rival systems of government were now fighting for supremacy.

117]

before Carthage's destruction. When Rome's self-defensive policy had depended upon the existence of outside threats to her security.

118]

run the Empire as a private estate. I do not wish to suggest that Caesar was blameless, but that in the circumstances in which his life was cast he had either to attach himself to one of the noble houses and depend upon their patronage for office, or deliberately to win the affection of the mob and thus make his own political way. Political life under noble patronage now allowed no scope at all; there was no movement for reform among any of the noble houses, and he would have had to 'toe the party line'. In so far as they were not viciously selfish, they were fossilized; power and privilege were everything, responsibility very little. Caesar, therefore, was forced to oppose the nobles if he wished to make a mark in political life, and to succeed he must be prepared to go to considerable lengths. The careers of Pompeius and Cicero show how the nobles treated their non-noble friends. It was almost impossible to help Rome as a nominee of the nobles.

by which alone the Republic could be saved. Cicero had far more understanding of the needs and dangers, but it was typical that because he was a *novus homo* he was used and despised by the nobles.

132]

deriving their sanction from the religion. One may compare the social function of religion in Victorian society, and the sanction which it gave to their ideals.

133]

their only claim to govern. Cf. Memmius' speech in Sullust, *Jug.* XXXI; Marius' speech, LXXXV, with its contemptuous contrast of the nobles and their Greek education with himself, a simple man who knew his job by apprenticeship in the field; his simple manners contrasted with their luxury; their love of drink instead of hard work. See also the speeches of Lepidus and Macer in the *Histories*; Macer, sec. 18, says: 'Ferant habeantque suo modo imperia, quaerant triumphos, Mithridatim, Sertorium et reliquias exulum cum imaginibus suis; absit periculum et labos quibus nulla pars fructus est.' Such jibes against the education, pride in ancestry, etc., of the nobles were a stock part of the popular attack from the outset, by people who were jealous of their power and unable to understand the spiritual and moral values of the class.

134]

defence of their privileges, not their code. A similar attack was made on the English governing class in the late nineteenth and twentieth centuries. The attack was directed at their wealth and exclusiveness; their code, which had guided them in building an empire, broadening the limits of civilization and maintaining a Pax Britannica for fifty years, became the object of contemptuous sneers. The 'public school code' and the 'old school tie' were mocked by all those who were taught to believe that they belonged to persons who could boast nothing but wealth and who rigorously excluded all others from their privileges. The critics did not add the benefits this class had brought to their country and to the world; that their labours enabled their country to flourish in unparalleled prosperity, and that their high ideals and scrupulous honesty earned them a universal respect. Their sense of mission was degraded to a cheap cat-call of Imperialism. And the class tended to react in the same way as did the Roman nobles.

to exercise it in their own interest. The Lex Domitia of 104 B.C. It is only proper to add that the first case of religious manipulation for purely political purposes seems to have been in 122 B.C., when on the strength of a nonsense story that wolves had torn up the boundary stones on the site of Carthage, where C. Gracchus was intending to settle colonists, the proposal, on the authority of the *pontifices*, was abandoned. It is significant and symbolical that it should have first appeared when the nobles were defending themselves against the Gracchi.

Caesar would not agree to trumps. During 59 B.C. his colleague, Bibulus, claimed that he was 'observing the heavens'; this meant that no legislation could be undertaken, and hence Caesar's laws were technically invalid.

135]

could never hope to compete. We may compare the appeal of Wesley and more particularly of Booth in England. Booth's appeal was to the wretched slum-dwelling workers, who had no reason to feel themselves part of society, and to whom the formal Christianity of the Churches made no appeal, since it was an integral part of the structure of society of which they were exiles (though in contradistinction to Rome, it was on the whole sincere, and reflected the rigid formality, the unchangeable framework of that society). Booth brought what was a *personal* message of hope and salvation to those who had none; he brought these people together, and by his social work and his provision of centres where they could meet together, he made small societies; he gave them roots, and with them a sense of confidence. Fortunately for England the religion he preached was Christianity, i.e. the religion of the society, but he emphasized the *personal* aspect of it, bringing a message to each individual. Had he brought some alien religion, he would have been equally successful, but the result to England would have been disastrous.

136]

could not be adequate for many at this time. We may compare the formality of the Church in Victorian times. In both cases the formality implied and in a sense reflected the structure of society; apart therefore from the political complications of the Roman religion, it could not appeal to those who were not an integral part of the society.

137]

would involve all equally. Cf. Momigliano, *J.R.S.* XXXI (1941), 156. When the Epicureans took an active part in Roman political life, chiefly after Caesar's murder, it was, I think, largely owing to the prevailing uncertainty. They had kept aloof before, because they were disgusted with public life, and found that the State was just sufficiently stable to allow them to lead their own lives without involving themselves in the corruption of politics. Later, Caesar seemed to guarantee a similar stability, and many therefore supported him.

But his death threatened even what stability there had been, and they were forced to take some part in order to restore, if possible, the security they needed. And since it was largely disgust with public life which kept them aloof and made them Epicureans, when the chance to be a Roman appeared and it seemed possible to fight for what they had given up as irretrievably lost, many, like Cassius, shed the cloak which had concealed their disappointment, and were ready to stand forth as Romans.

of which Rome stood in such sore need. I do not wholly agree with Momigliano's final paragraph, p. 157. I think the Imperial writers were probably right in not conceding much to Epicureanism in the fight for liberty, because it was not Epicureanism but its denial that made the so-called Epicureans fight. They had embraced it as an escape, they abandoned it when they saw the chance to act; and, as M. points out, when their hopes were disappointed, they relapsed once more into quiescence and acquiescence. Nor do I think that Epicureanism gave spirituality to the Roman peace; it had represented a passive surrender; the Stoics fought for principles; not so the Epicureans; the spirituality of Horace and Virgil came not from Epicureanism but from their religious instinct and faith combined with Stoicism.

139]

fundamental to the welfare of the State. This is very important. See Cicero, *De Harus. Resp.* IX, 19; *De Nat. Deorum*, II, 3, 8; III, 2, 5. Cicero's attitude in this important matter shows how keenly he felt the necessity of a common religion to bind society together, and this attitude corresponds exactly with Varro's. It is idle in this connexion to refer to Cicero's speculation on the gods and his philosophical theories; one may speculate without calling in question one's belief. Ennius could write his *Euhemerus* without introducing a spirit of scepticism; we may compare the theological battles concerning the Trinity and the nature of Christ. Kroll has rightly distinguished between Religion and Religiosität (*Kultur d. Ciceronischen Zeit*, II, 1 ff.), one's religious beliefs and one's speculations about religion; those who discuss Cicero's thought too often suppose that they have defined his belief, in the same way as those who describe the religious atmosphere of the early second century suppose that they have demonstrated a scepticism at that time by referring to the *Euhemerus* and odd fragments from Ennius' tragedies (which, in any case, out of their context are worthless for the purpose).

142]

rejoicing at their success. See, for instance, Cicero's description in *Pro Plancio*, VIII, 19 ff. The liveliness of this sentiment seems attested by Cicero's discussion of dual citizenship, *De Legibus*, II, 2, 5; he is clearly here aiming to bring facts into line with his hopes and ideals of Rome. At the time that he wrote this, the local patriotism was there, but not the broader one; that did not come until Augustus.

143]

had yet been lit. The apathy shown by Italy when the Civil War broke out, even where a *patronus* might have claimed support, indicates the extent to which the Italians were unconcerned in Roman squabbles, and felt that whatever happened there, they were losing nothing. Cf. Syme, *op. cit.* 69, 286 ff.

144]

allow her to fulfil her mission. It is in this sense no less than in the political sense that Rome now ceased to be a city-state. More and more Rome's contribution to the world came not from its local citizens but from her Empire. The city-state had been the cradle of the ideas and ideals which Italy had raised to manhood and now gave to the Roman world through Rome as the Imperial capital; and this capital now belonged to the whole Roman world, not only to its citizens; in this new role she was eventually to win the love and respect of all within that Empire, as *their* capital and the embodiment of *their* ideals. Rome ceased to be the private possession of those who dwelt there, and was given to the Empire and the world.

151]

crude or vulgar poems. Ovid's flippant and salacious writings reveal an outlook different from Horace's; but Ovid was not an Augustan in this sense. Born in 43 B.C., he had not known at first hand the horror of civil war; he grew up into the peace and pleasure of Augustan Rome and became a member of the pleasure-seeking, immoral circles that a large city is liable to foster, particularly at a time of relaxation from so long a strain. The Augustan Age ended before the death of Augustus, yet even so Ovid ended his days at Tomi.

154]

turned his mind towards the past. I am taking his works not in the order of composition but in chronological order. He began with his own time, the *Catilina*, then sought the origin for its troubles in the *Jugurtha*, and finally wrote the *Histories*, in which the good start made by Marius and his supporters was frustrated by the *dominatio* of Sulla, which restored the *status quo ante*.

none but the most general moral terms. It is indicative of Sallust's limited powers of penetration that to his understanding the problem from the time of Jugurtha to his own day remained the same and at the same level, with luxury, etc., as the causes. The degeneration had begun with the destruction of Carthage (*Cat.* 10), and so far as one can see could, in Sallust's estimation, have been arrested at any time by moral legislation. Even the political problems are reduced—or raised—to simple moral ones; it is a deep contrast to Thucydides' understanding.

156]

accept as genuine his Letters to Caesar. I do not intend to add further to the literature on this subject; I accept as genuine both the *Letters to Caesar* and the *Invective against Cicero*. For the most convenient summary of the bibliography on the subject in English, see Fraenkel, *J.R.S.* XLI (1951), 192 ff. No one has succeeded in raising more than doubts as to their genuineness on historical grounds—indeed, even where not accepted as Sallustian, they are generally made near-contemporary; and some, at least, of these doubts are only so to us who live after the events and know what the answer was; but a person living in the midst of the uncertainty and chaos of the times might well have formed judgements about persons and events which the future showed to be wrong. Such judgements cannot fairly be used in an attempt to prove that the letters are not genuine; one has only to reflect how difficult it would have been to write such a composition in Germany in 1943 to realize the untrustworthiness of such arguments. Fraenkel, in the article referred to, states categorically that the letters are not Sallustian, basing his statement on the fact that their style is Sallustian, and that in such a composition he would not have used the style in which he wrote his historical works. This, too, I cannot accept; the basis of his argument is that there was a certain style proper to history, that Sallust studied it carefully and used it, and that he would have similarly used the pamphleteering style when writing a pamphlet. This is to a certain extent true if we assume that a man wrote merely according to a conventional style; but it implies a considerable artificiality, by which I mean that Sallust is made to turn it on, as it were, for historical writing. This is to make of his style something too superficial; Latte, *Sallust*, has properly shown the relation of the style to the man, and points out that he used the style to express *himself* (p. 56). This, as I have shown, is my own view; I do not think one will properly understand Sallust or his works unless one realizes the close connexion between the two; *le style, c'est l'homme* is more true of Sallust than of many other writers. And the connexion between the historical works of Sallust and the *Letters* is much closer than Fraenkel allows; as I have tried to show, his historical works were the result of his deep and restless dissatisfaction with the spiritual and political chaos of his times; it was to explain this that he wrote his historical works; they are all charged with the passion of the present. And the *Letters* are equally concerned with the present, consisting of suggestions how to put things right to the one man he thought capable of the task. In other words, all his works represent his mental struggle with the present; they are thus all equally historical or non-historical, and

Sallust is expressing himself equally in all of them. Granted the influences which helped to form his style, the style when formed represented Sallust, not rhetorical theory.

in the preceding years. As he himself says, *Hist.* frag. 11: optumis autem moribus ex maxima concordia egit populus Romanus inter secundum et tertium bellum Carthaginiense.

157]

literary indebtedness to him. Sincere admiration of a person frequently involves imitation of that which commands the admiration. A writer's views and his style are closely connected, as jointly the expression of the character; admiration of the one tends to involve admiration of the other.

158]

Bombastic and verbose it seemed. Cf. Tacitus, *Dialogus*, 18: satis constat ne Ciceroni quidem obtrectatores defuisse, quibus inflatus et tumens, nec satis pressus sed supra modum exsultans et superfluens et parum Atticus videretur.

159]

move away to other sport. As, ironically, tended to happen with the second-rate 'Atticists', according to Cicero, *Brutus*, XXVIII, 9. But Cicero was an interested party, and perhaps not wholly impartial.

Cicero himself attests. The fact that a similar movement was in progress in Greece was not in itself the reason for the movement at Rome. Rome was by now sufficiently mature to make up her own mind on such matters; but feeling the need they naturally turned once again to their *exemplaria Graeca.* They did not affect the style simply because Greece had begun to turn to Lysias and Thucydides; but once granted the psychological need, the rhetorical teachers of the Greek world naturally exercised a great influence on their pupils.

162]

the Roman's proper philosophy. Much has been written to show the debt of the Romans to Panaetius and Poseidonius, but it is almost equally true that these two men owed a great debt to Rome. They succeeded because they adapted their Stoicism to suit Romans; they made the concessions, not Rome; Romans remained firmly Roman, and what ran counter to their beliefs and *ethos* they rejected. It is therefore almost as true to say that these two men became Roman as that the Romans became Stoics.

rejected as non-Roman. This is not to say that he did not have an influence, just as did Caesar; but odes became Horatian, and love poetry found its outlet in erotic elegy which was very different in spirit from Catullus' love poems.

CHRONOLOGICAL TABLE

B.C.	HISTORICAL EVENTS	B.C.	LITERARY EVENTS
		207	Hymn composed by Livius Andronicus.
		204	Ennius brought to Rome by Cato.
202	Defeat of Hannibal at Zama.	*c.* 202	Fabius Pictor publishes his history of Rome.
200–197	Second Macedonian War against Philip V.		
		c. 198	Death of Naevius.
		c. 194	Birth of Terence.
193–188	War against Antiochus the Great of Syria.		
186	*Senatus Consultum de Bacchanalibus.*		
		184	Death of Plautus.
180	*Lex Villia Annalis*, fixing legal age for holding of different magistracies.	180	Birth of Lucilius.
177	Tib. Sempronius Gracchus in Sardinia.		
171–167	Third Macedonian War against Perseus.		
167	Epirus plundered and enslaved.	167	Polybius comes to Rome.
		166–159	Production of Terence's comedies
161	Expulsion of Greek philosophers and teachers from Rome.		
		c. 159	Death of Terence.
155	Athenian embassy, including Carneades, at Rome.		
153–133	War in Spain.		
149–146	Third Punic War.		
149	*Lex Calpurnia de pecuniis repetundis*, establishing first permanent court at Rome for trial of extortion in provinces.	*c.* 149	Publication of Cato's *Origines.*
147	War with Achaean League.		
146	Destruction of Carthage and Corinth.		
		135	Panaetius at Rome.
133	Destruction of Numantia.		
133	Tribunate of Tiberius Gracchus. Attalus III of Pergamum bequeathes his kingdom to Rome. Death of Tib. Gracchus.		
		132	Lucilius begins his writing.
123	First tribunate of Caius Gracchus.		

Chronological Table

HISTORICAL EVENTS		LITERARY EVENTS	
B.C.		B.C.	
122	Second tribunate of C. Gracchus.		
121	Death of C. Gracchus. First use of *senatus consultum ultimum.*		
118	Death of Micipsa, king of Numidia.		
116	Roman commission sent to Numidia.	116	Birth of the scholar, M. Terentius Varro.
113	Fighting against Cimbri.		
112	War declared against Jugurtha.		
111	Peace made with Jugurtha, who is summoned to Rome. War renewed.		
110	Judicial commission instituted on motion of C. Mamilius, condemns unsuccessful Roman generals.		
107	Marius' first consulship. Defeat of Romans by Cimbri and Teutoni.		
106	End of Jugurthine War.	106	Birth of Cicero.
105	Roman defeat by Cimbri and Teutoni at Arausio.		
102	Marius, consul for fourth time, defeats Teutoni at Aquae Sextiae.	102	Death of Lucilius.
101	Marius, consul for fifth time, defeats Cimbri near Vercellae.		
100	Sixth consulship of Marius; Saturninus tribune, Glaucia praetor. Riots and death of Saturninus and Glaucia.	100	*Floruit* of Q. Lutatius Catulus. Birth of C. Julius Caesar.
		c. 96	Birth of Lucretius.
92	Condemnation and exile of P. Rutilius Rufus.	92	Suppression of Latin *rhetores*.
91	Tribunate of M. Livius Drusus. Murder of Drusus.		
91–89	Social War.		
		c. 90	Poseidonius begins teaching at Rhodes.
88	L. Cornelius Sulla consul, P. Sulpicius Rufus tribune. *Leges Sulpiciae*. March on Rome by Sulla.		
88–84	First Mithridatic War.		
87	L. Cornelius Cinna consul. Return of Marius and Marian massacre. Cinna permanently consul 87–84.	87	Birth of Catullus.
		86	Birth of Sallust.
83–82	Return of Sulla; civil war; Sullan proscriptions.		
81	Sulla *dictator legibus scribundis et rei publicae constituendae*.		

Chronological Table

B.C.	HISTORICAL EVENTS	B.C.	LITERARY EVENTS
79	Sulla resigns dictatorship.		
77	Pompeius given chief command against Sertorius.		
74–65	Second Mithridatic War.		
70	Consulship of Pompeius and Crassus.	70	The Verrine orations of Cicero. Birth of Virgil.
67	*Lex Gabinia*, giving Pompeius the command against the pirates.		
66	*Lex Manilia*, conferring on Pompeius the command against Mithridates. First Catilinarian conspiracy.		
		65	Birth of Horace.
63	Cicero consul. Second Catilinarian conspiracy.		
62	Pompeius' return to Italy.		
59	C. Julius Caesar consul; first Triumvirate. Caesar given provinces of Gallia Cisalpina and Narbonensis for five years.	59	Birth of Livy (died A.D. 17).
58	Banishment of Cicero (recalled in following year).		
56	Conference at Lucca.		
55	Pompeius and Crassus consuls; Pompeius receives both provinces of Spain, Crassus Syria, for five years; Caesar confirmed in provinces for further five years.		
		c. 54	Death of Catullus.
53	Defeat and death of Crassus at Carrhae.		
52	Pompeius sole consul.	*c.* 52	Death of Lucretius.
		51	Publication of Cicero's *De Republica*, and of Caesar's *Commentarii de Bello Gallico*.
49	Caesar crosses Rubicon.		
48	Battle of Pharsalus and death of Pompeius.		
46	Caesar given dictatorship for ten years.		
45	Caesar made *dictator perpetuus*.		
44	Death of Caesar. Arrival of C. Octavius in Italy.	44	Cicero still at work on *De Legibus*.
		43	Death of Cicero. Birth of Ovid.
42	Campaign of Philippi; deaths of Brutus and Cassius.		
		40	Virgil's *Fourth Eclogue*.
		35	Death of Sallust.

Chronological Table

	HISTORICAL EVENTS		LITERARY EVENTS
B.C.		B.C.	
32	Declaration of war against Cleopatra.		
31	Battle of Actium.		
30	Deaths of Antonius and Cleopatra.	30	Virgil's *Georgics* completed.
		29	Livy begins the composition of his history.
27	First settlement of Augustus.		
23	Second settlement of Augustus.	23	First three books of Horace's *Odes* published.
		19	Death of Virgil.
		17	Publication of *Aeneid*.
		13	Publication of fourth book of Horace's *Odes*.
A.D. 14	Death of Augustus.		

SELECT BIBLIOGRAPHY

I. GENERAL

(*a*) History

ADCOCK, F. E. *The Roman Art of War under the Republic.* Cambridge, Mass., 1940.

BLOCH and CARCOPINO. *Histoire Romaine*, vol. II. Paris, 1935–6.

BROUGHTON, T. R. S. *The Magistrates of the Roman Republic*, 2 vols. New York, 1951–3.

Cambridge Ancient History, vols. VIII and IX. Cambridge, 1930–2.

CARY, M. *A History of Rome.* London, 1935.

DRUMANN, W. *Geschichte Roms in seinem Übergange von der republikanischen zur monarchischen Verfassung*, 2nd ed. by P. Groebe, 5 vols. Leipzig, 1899–1929.

FRANK, T. *Roman Imperialism*, 2nd ed. New York, 1925.

HEITLAND, W. E. *Agricola.* Cambridge, 1921.

HILL, H. *The Roman Middle Class.* Oxford, 1952.

HOMO, L. *Primitive Italy and the Rise of Roman Imperialism.* London, 1927.

HOMO, L. *Roman Political Institutions.* London, 1929.

MAGIE, D. *Roman Rule in Asia Minor*, 2 vols. Princeton, 1950.

MÜNZER, F. *Römische Adelsparteien und Adelsfamilien.* Stuttgart, 1920.

PIGANIOL, A. *Histoire de Rome*, 3rd ed. Paris, 1954.

SHERWIN WHITE, A. N. *The Roman Citizenship.* Oxford, 1939.

SIBER, H. *Römische Verfassungsrecht.* Leipzig, 1952.

(*b*) Literature

BARDON, H. *La Littérature Latine inconnue*, vol. I. Paris, 1952.

BICKEL, E. *Lehrbuch der Geschichte der römischen Literatur.* Heidelberg, 1937.

BIGNONE, E. *Storia della Letteratura Latina*, 3 vols. Florence, 1945–50.

COUSIN, J. *Études sur la Poésie latine.* Paris, 1945.

DUFF, J. WIGHT. *A Literary History of Rome to the Close of the Golden Age*, 3rd ed. revised by A. M. Duff. London, 1953.

FUNAIOLI, G. *Studi di Letteratura antica*, 2 vols. Bologna, 1949.

LAISTNER, M. L. W. *The Greater Roman Historians.* California, 1947.

NORDEN, E. *Antike Kunstprosa*, 2 vols. Leipzig, 1898.

PARATORE, E. *Storia della Letteratura Latina.* Florence, 1951.

ROSTAGNI, A. *La Letteratura di Roma Repubblicana ed Augustea.* Bologna, 1939.

ROSTAGNI, A. *Letteratura Latina*, vol. I. Turin, 1949.

SCHANZ-HOSIUS. *Geschichte der römischen Literatur*, vol. I. Munich, 1927.

TEUFFEL, W. S. *Geschichte der römischen Literatur*, revised by Kroll and Skutsch, vols. I and II. Leipzig, 1916–20.

(c) THOUGHT AND RELIGION

ALTHEIM, F. *History of Roman Religion*. London, 1938.

BAILEY, C. *Phases in the Religion of Ancient Rome*. Berkley, Cal., 1932.

BAILEY, C. *Religion in Virgil*. Oxford, 1935.

BARTH-GOLDECKEMEYER. *Die Stoa*. Stuttgart, 1946.

CARCOPINO, J. *Aspects mystiques de la Rome paienne*, 6th ed. Paris, 1942.

FOWLER, W. WARDE. *The Religious Experiences of the Roman People*. London, 1911.

FOWLER, W. WARDE. *Roman Ideas of Deity*. London, 1914.

FUCHS, H. *Der geistige Widerstand gegen Rom in der Antiken Welt*. Berlin, 1938.

MEYER, ERNST. *Römischer Staat und Staatsgedanke*. Zürich, 1948.

POHLENZ, M. *Die Stoa*, 2 vols. Göttingen, 1948.

REINHARD, K. *Kosmos und Sympathie*. Munich, 1926.

STANKE, R. *Die Politische Philosophie des Althertums*. Vienna, 1951.

TURCHI, N. *La Religione di Roma antica*. Bologna, 1939.

II. PRE-GRACCHAN PERIOD

(a) HISTORY

ADCOCK, F. E. 'Delenda est Carthago.' *Camb. Hist. Journ.* XIII, 1946, pp. 117 ff.

DE SANCTIS, G. *Storia dei Romani*, vol. IV, 1. Turin, 1923.

GELZER, M. *Die Nobilität der römischen Republik*. Leipzig, 1912.

HOLLEAUX, M. *Rome, la Grèce et les monarchies hellénistiques*. Paris, 1921.

MCDONALD, A. H. and WALBANK, F. W. 'The Origins of the Second Macedonian War.' *J.R.S.* XXVII, 1937, 180 ff.

MCDONALD, A. H. 'Scipio Africanus and Roman Politics in the Second Century B.C.' *J.R.S.* XXVIII, 1938, 153 ff.

MCDONALD, A. H. 'The History of Rome and Italy in the Second Century B.C.' *Camb. Hist. Journ.* VI, 1939, 124 ff.

MCDONALD, A. H. 'Rome and the Italian Confederation.' *J.R.S.* XXXIV, 1944, 11 ff.

MARMORALE, E. V. *Cato Maior*, 2nd ed. Bari, 1949.

SCULLARD, H. H. *Roman Politics 220–150 B.C.* Oxford, 1951.

SCULLARD, H. H. *History of the Roman World, 753–146 B.C.*, 2nd ed. London, 1951.

STEVENSON, G. H. *Roman Provincial Administration*. Oxford, 1939.

SUTHERLAND, C. H. V. *The Romans in Spain.* London, 1939.
WALBANK, F. W. *Philip V of Macedon.* Cambridge, 1940.
WILLEMS, P. *Le Sénat de la République romaine, sa Composition et ses Attributions,* 2 vols. Louvain, 1883–5.

(*b*) LITERATURE AND THOUGHT

COLIN, G. *Rome et la Grèce de 200 à 146 avant J.C.* Paris, 1905.
DE SANCTIS, G. *Storia dei Romani,* vol. IV, 2, pt. I. Florence, 1953.
DUDLEY, D. R. 'Blossius of Cumae.' *J.R.S.* XXXI, 1941, 94 ff.
FRANK, T. *Life and Letters in the Roman Republic.* Cambridge, 1930.
HEINZE, R. *Virgils epische Technik,* 4th ed. Leipzig, 1928.
LEO, F. *Geschichte der römischen Literatur,* vol. I. Berlin, 1913.
MARMORALE, E. V. *Naevius Poeta,* 2nd ed. Firenze, 1950.
NORDEN, E. *Ennius und Virgilius.* Leipzig, 1915.
STEWART, E. M. *The Annals of Ennius.* Cambridge, 1925.
VALMAGGI, L. *I Frammenti degli Annali.* Turin, 1900.
VAN STRAATEN, M. *Panaetii Rhodii Fragmenta.* Leiden, 1952.

III. POST-GRACCHAN PERIOD

(*a*) HISTORY

BENNETT, H. *Cinna and his Times.* Menasha, 1923.
CARCOPINO, J. *Autour des Graccques: Études critiques.* Paris, 1928.
CARCOPINO, J. *Sylla: ou la Monarchie manquée,* 2nd ed. Paris, 1950.
CARDINALI, G. *Studi Graccani.* Genoa, 1912.
CIACERI, E. *Cicerone e i suoi Tempi,* 2 vols., 2nd ed. Milan-Rome-Naples 1939–41.
COBBAN, J. M. *Senate and Provinces, 78–49 B.C.* Cambridge, 1935.
FRACCARO, P. 'Studi sull' età dei Gracchi.' *Studi storici per l'antichità classica,* V, 1912, 317 ff.; VI, 1913, 42 ff.
FRACCARO, P. 'Ricerche su Gaio Graccho.' *Athenaeum,* n.s. III, 1925, 76 ff.
GELZER, M. *Cäsar der Politiker und Staatsman,* 2nd ed. Stuttgart and Berlin, 1941.
GELZER, M. *Pompeius.* Munich, 1949.
GREENIDGE, A. H. J. *A History of Rome from the Tribunate of Tiberius Gracchus to the End of the Jugurthine War, 133–104 B.C.* London, 1904.
HEITLAND, W. E. *The Roman Republic,* vols. II and III. Cambridge, 1909.
HOLMES, T. RICE. *The Roman Republic,* 3 vols. Oxford, 1923.
MARSH, F. B. *History of the Roman World from 146 to 30 B.C.,* 2nd ed. revised by H. H. Scullard. London, 1952.

Meyer, Ed. *Cäsars Monarchie und das Principat des Pompeius*, 2nd ed. Berlin, 1919.

Meyer, Ed. 'Untersuchungen zur Geschichte der Gracchen.' *Kleine Schriften*, vol. I, 2nd ed., 363 ff. Halle, 1924.

Oman, C. *Seven Roman Statesmen*. London, 1923.

Paribeni, R. *L'Età di Cesare e di Augusto*. Bologna, 1950.

Passerini, A. 'Caio Mario come uomo politico.' *Athenaeum*, n.s. XII, 1934, 10 ff.; 109 ff.; 257 ff.; 340 ff.

Passerini, A. *Caio Mario*. Rome, 1941.

Robinson, F. W. *Marius, Saturninus und Glaucia*. Bonn, 1912.

Seymour, P. A. 'The Policy of Livius Drusus the Younger.' *Eng. Hist. Rev.* vol. XXIX, 1914, 147 ff.

Syme, R. *The Roman Revolution*. Oxford, 1939.

Taylor, L. R. *Party Politics in the Age of Caesar*. Berkeley, 1949.

(*b*) Literature and Thought

Cumont, F. *Les Religions orientales dans le Paganisme romain*, 4th ed. Paris, 1929.

Cumont, F. *Lux Perpetua*. Paris, 1949.

Fowler, W. Warde. *Social Life at Rome in the Age of Cicero*. London, 1908.

Heinze, R. *Die augusteische Kultur*. Berlin, 1933.

Kroll, W. *Die Kultur der ciceronischen Zeit*, 2 vols. Leipzig, 1933.

Reinhardt, K. *Poseidonios*. Munich, 1921.

Sellar, W. Y. *The Roman Poets of the Republic*. Oxford, 1889.

Vogt, J. *Ciceros Glaube an Rom*. Stuttgart, 1935.

von Fritz, K. 'Sallust and the Attitude of the Roman Nobility at the time of the Wars against Jugurtha.' *T.A.P.A.* LXXIV, 1943, 132 ff.

Wirszubski, C. *Libertas as a Political Idea at Rome*. Cambridge, 1950.

INDEX

Index